MY FORBIDDEN FACE

MY FORBIDDEN FACE

Growing up under the Taliban:
a young woman's story

Latifa
with the collaboration of
Chékéha Hachemi

Translated by Lisa Appignanesi

Virago

A *Virago* Book
First published by Virago Press 2002

Copyright © 2002 Editions Robert Editions Carrière
Translation copyright © 2002 Lisa Appignanesi
International Rights Management: Susanna Lea Associates, Paris

A CIP catalogue record for this book is available
from the British Library.

ISBN 1 86049 956 2

Typeset in Garamond
by Palimpsest Book Production Limited,
Polmont, Stirlingshire

Printed and bound in Australia
by Griffin Press

Virago
An imprint of
Time Warner Books UK
Brettenham House
Lancaster Place
London WC2E 7EN

www.virago.co.uk

Life always comes to an end.
There is no need to be oppressed.
If submission is the condition of my life,
I have no need of this life
In slavery.
It can rain showers of gold
And I'll say to the sky
There is no need of this rain.

This book talks of past and recent events in the life of my family in Afghanistan, my country.

I hope it will serve as a key for other women, those whose speech has been padlocked and who have buried their testimony in their hearts or their memories.

I dedicate this book to all those Afghani girls and women who have kept their dignity until their last breath; to those women who have been deprived of their rights in their country, and who live in obscurity, despite the fact that we are in the twenty-first century; to all those executed in public, without trial and without pity, and under the eyes of their children and loved ones.

I dedicate it, also, to my mother who helped me at each step of the way by giving me lessons in freedom and resistance.

Latifa

Acknowledgements

My profound gratitude is due to the following:

Elle magazine, whose help made a decisive difference when, in May 2001, we fled Afghanistan to come to France, and in particular to Marie-Françoise Colombani, who champions our cause with great conviction, and to Valerie Toranian;

Chékéba Hachemi, who collaborated in the writing of this book and who has dedicated her life to the cause of Afghani women. The association she created in France, Afghanistan Libre, gathers funds destined for the building of schools and hospitals in our country;

Hakim Said, who helped me to translate my thoughts into French.

I also wish warmly to thank Mr and Mrs Masstan and all my friends for their constant encouragement.

To send contributions to Afghanistan Libre:

80 Avenue Aristide-Briand
92150 Antony
France
Tel: 33 1 42 72 16 43
Fax: 33 46 68 58 55
afghanlibre@hotmail.com
CCP La Source-4060 932 X
www.afghanistan-libre.org
See also www.rawa.fancymarketing.net
This is the home page of the Revolutionary Association of the Women of Afghanistan

Contents

A Brief Chronology

1747 Creation of the Afghan state.

1919 Third Anglo–Afghan war secures Independence of Afghanistan.

1921 The Treaty of Kabul puts an end to British and Russian claims on Afghanistan.

1933–73 Reign of King Mohammed Zaher Shah.

1959 Wearing of the veil becomes optional.

1964 Women are given the right to vote.

1965 First Parliamentary elections.

1973 The monarchy is overthrown by Mohammed Daoud who institutes the First Republic of Afghanistan of which he becomes President.

April 1978 A coup d'état puts into place the Second Republic which is Communist. Noor Mohammed Taraki is the president and Hafizullah Amin the prime minister. The reforms imposed on Afghan Society, which has remained largely traditional until this point, bring popular uprisings in their wake, many of these Islamic and tribal in origin and destabilise the regime.

December 1979 Soviet Military Intervention. The Mujahidin Resistance engages in a guerilla war against the Soviet

Army and the Afghan Army under its control. This lasts for ten years.

1979–86 Presidency of Babrak Karmal.

1986–92 Presidency of Dr Najibullah.

April 1988 Signature of the Geneva Accords under the aegis of the United Nations, by the Kabul Government, the Soviet Union, Pakistan and the United States, which put a timetable to the retreat of the Soviet Army.

February 1989 End of the evacuation of Soviet troops. Beginning of the civil war between Mujahidin of different ethnic groups, notably the Tajik, Ahmed Shah Massoud, and the Pashtun, Gulbuddin Hekmatyar.

March 1992 The troops of Commander Massoud take over the northern provinces.

April 1992 Massoud's Mujahidin take over Kabul. The Islamic State of Afghanistan is proclaimed. Sebghatullah Modjaddedi becomes president for two months and is then replaced by Burhanuddin Rabbani in June. Civil War begins again between the forces of Commander Massoud and extremist Islamist fighters supported by Pakistan. These 'Taliban' win their first victory in the south when they take over Kandahar in 1994.

1994 Rise of the Taliban, with Pakistani and Saudi support.

September 1995 The Taliban take Herat.

September 1996 The Taliban take Jalalabad and Kabul.

1997–8 The Taliban advance into the north. Several times they take and lose the city of Mazar-e-Sharif. Their victory is effective in August 1998. Commander Massoud withdraws to the Valley of Panshir and is the sole active opponent of the Taliban Regime.

9 September 2001 Ahmed Shah Massoud is the victim of an assassination attempt. On 13 September his death is officially announced.

11 September 2001 Islamist forces, with Afghan backing, attack New York and Washington.

7 October 2001 Beginning of American and Allied military attacks on Afghanistan.

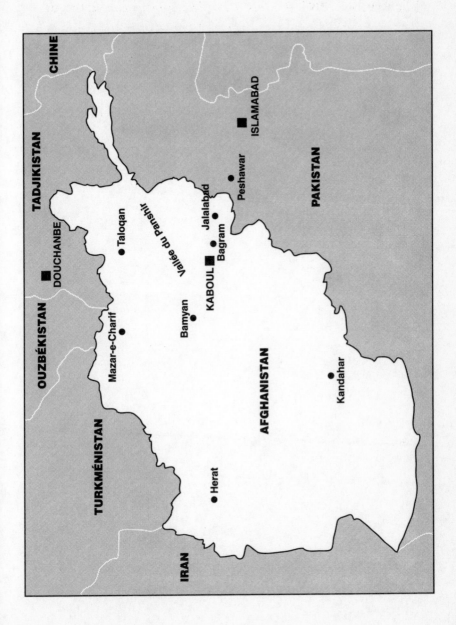

1

The White Flag on the Mosque

27 September 1996, 9.00 a.m. Someone knocks violently at the front door. The entire family jumps. We've been in a nervous state since dawn. My father walks hastily out of the room. My anxious mother follows him with her eyes. Her features are drawn in fatigue. She hasn't slept all night. No one has slept. The rocket fire around the city went on until two in the morning. My sister, Soraya, and I whispered in the dark. We didn't stop even once it had grown quiet. There was no real rest to be found anywhere.

You'd think that in Kabul we'd have grown used to being rocket targets. I'm sixteen and I'm convinced I've always heard them. The city's been encircled for so very long. It's been attacked and bombarded and attacked again. Murderous gangs have set us on fire and smoked us out, sometimes sent us running down to the distant cellar for shelter. One more night of upheaval should be just part of the routine.

But today feels different.

Father comes back into the kitchen. Right behind him is our young cousin, Farad. He's breathless and a ghastly colour and looks as if he's shivering on the inside. His whole face is fear. He has trouble speaking, the words fall all over each other interspersed with strange gasps.

'I came . . . to get your news. Is everything OK? You didn't see anything? You don't know anything? But they're here! Yes, they've taken Kabul. The Taliban are in Kabul. Didn't they bang on your door? Didn't they demand all your arms?'

'No. No one came,' my father mutters. 'But we saw the white flag blowing above the mosque. We've been fearing the worst. Daoud saw it this morning.'

This morning at about five when he went down as usual to fetch water from the building's communal tap, my young brother, Daoud, rushed back up quickly, the bucket in his hand still empty. 'I saw a white flag on the mosque and another on the school!'

The flag of the Taliban. It had never yet fluttered above Kabul. I've only ever seen it on television or in newspaper photographs.

We knew the Taliban were close. It was repeated around town that they held a position only some ten or fifteen kilometres away from the capital. But no one really thought they'd get as far as this. As far as Kabul. We kept trying to find some news on radio or television, but there was nothing. Nothing at all. We've had neither sound nor image since six o'clock last night. This morning, my father tried once more to reach the rest of the family in Kabul. But all in vain. The telephone was still dead.

Nervously, I fiddle with the knob on the radio. It's meant to work on batteries, but it only crackles. Neither Radio Kabul, the local station, nor the BBC, nor the Voice of America, which I look for on the off-chance, manifest themselves . . . If Farad hadn't dared to cycle like a madman to get here, to cover those two dangerous kilometres which separate our neighbourhoods, we would still have no news, nothing apart from those billowing white flags.

What Farad has seen is so terrifying he's rendered almost dumb. Then suddenly, everything pours out of him in one long breathless exclamation.

'They've hung President Najibullah and his brother on Ariana Square . . . It's hideous. Horrible.'

He addresses my father, then Daoud, all the time staring at us women in anguish. Terrible things are said about what the Taliban have done to women in the regions they've already occupied. I've never seen Farad so agitated, his eyes gleaming with fear.

'Can you imagine? President Najibullah! They hung him with plastic pipes. There are lots of people on the square. They're forcing people to look . . . to stare. Beating them. I saw them.'

The five of us have turned to stone. We can't find anything to say in response.

Since the early morning, despite the white flags reported by my brother, I've been in denial. The government forces must have pulled back only to retrench and do battle again, I tell myself. They've merely taken momentary refuge a little further north, in another suburb of the city. The Mujahidin couldn't have abandoned Kabul.

I've heard and read so much about the Taliban that I want to ignore the reports, pretend they're not true. Radio Kabul has told us they're locking up the women, preventing them from going to work or school. Women don't have lives anymore. The Taliban take away daughters, burn peasants' houses, enlist men by force. The Taliban want to destroy our country.

Yesterday life was still 'normal' in Kabul, despite the ruins and the civil war. Yesterday, I went to the dressmaker's with my sister to try on the dresses we were to wear at a wedding that was to take place today. There would have been music. We would have danced.

Life can't just stop like this on 27 September 1996! I'm sixteen and there's still so much to do – get through my entrance exam for a journalism course at university, for one thing. No, it's altogether impossible that the Taliban will stay in Kabul. This is just a temporary setback.

I hear my father arguing with Daoud, but I only take in bits of their conversation because I'm so upset.

'Najibullah's a Pashtun, just like them. It's mad that they're taking it out on a fellow Pashtun. And they seized him in the United Nations Building. Then they hung him. It doesn't make any sense.'

My father, too, is a Pashtun, the dominant ethnic group in our country. Like many others, he thought that if by some misfortune the Taliban invaded the capital, they'd certainly round up Najibullah, not in order to hang him, but to liberate him and to propose that he participate in their new government.

The Kabulis don't like Najibullah much, our one-time head of government. He's a man who can move from one side to the other as easily as the drug and arms traffickers move across the border with Pakistan. My father judges him harshly and thinks he's a traitor to our country, corrupt and criminal. Najibullah was the head of the Afghan

Communist Secret Service, the Khad, our very own and sinister equivalent of the Soviet KGB. At the time of the last coup in April 1992, when the Resistance laid siege to Kabul, he simply fled. The army caught up with him at the airport where he was about to get on a plane bound for some foreign destination. When they forced him to stay, he took refuge in the UN building not far from Ariana Square, and he hasn't come out since. Until today, that is.

I was still a child when President Najibullah made a speech calling for reconciliation between the various sides of the Resistance. He stood on the very square where Farad just saw him hanging. If the Taliban can go and get a former president out of the United Nations headquarters in Kabul, that can only mean that terror and chaos are now our rulers.

My cousin Farad is still in a state of shock. He's worried about his parents, too, and doesn't want to stay away from home for too long.

'If you have to go out, Uncle, take care. I've seen them hitting people with huge whips. They're terrifying, dressed like Pakistanis in long floppy trousers. They're parading round in pick-ups, and only stop at random to beat people in the crowd – especially anyone without a beard. And you haven't got a beard.'

Farad doesn't have one either. Does one grow a beard when one's a sixteen-year-old in jeans and trainers? A sixteen-year-old, like so many others, who listens to rock and dreams along to the sentimental Indian love stories we like to read.

The Taliban all wear beards. They state that beards have to be as long as a hand. They never wear a pakol, which is our traditional Afghan beret, sign of the Resistance. A lot of them aren't Afghani, or even Pashtun. Pakistan supports them and recruits them abroad. The pictures we see on television and the reports from witnesses in the Taliban-occupied provinces attest to that: in their ranks there are lots of Pakistanis, but also Arabs who've come from various other Muslim countries. The majority of them don't even speak our language.

My father's watching the street from the terrace of our apartment. The neighbourhood is quiet. The Taliban flag is still floating gently above the mosque. But in our heads there's a storm. We look at each other. Farad quickly swallows a glass of hot tea. Father comes in from the terrace and shakes his head. He can't make himself believe that the Taliban have really hung Najibullah.

This morning my father and I won't go jogging with our dog, Bingo. This morning, Father's asking himself a thousand silent questions. He keeps them to himself because he doesn't want to trouble Mother any more than she already is after the ordeal of seventeen long years of war. War, fighting, that's all I've known, really, since my birth on the first day of spring, 20 March 1980. But even under the Soviets, even under the rocket fire of enemy factions, even amidst the ruins, we still lived freely in Kabul.

What kind of life will my father be able to offer his family now? What kind of fate awaits his children? I've had the good fortune to be born into a loving and united family, at once religious and liberal. My oldest sister, Chakila, is married and lives, as custom would have it, with her parents-in-law. They're in Pakistan and she's waiting for her husband to send for her from the United States where he is. Soraya, who's twenty, is single and for the last three years, has worked as a flight attendant on Air Ariana. She came home the day before yesterday from her regular Dubai run and was meant to leave again this morning. Daoud is an economics student, and I, well, I've just passed the first part of the exam which will enable me to become a journalist. That's what I've always wanted to be. My father and my entire family have been hoping that I'd succeed in my studies, become a reporter, and travel the country to earn my keep. Can all that have changed from one second to the next?

I need to go to Ariana Square to see what's happening. So does my sister. We have to see to believe. To believe that the Taliban really are here in our city, that they've really hung Najibullah and his brother, that the catastrophe whose reality I refused to consider until yesterday is now actually upon us. My elder brother, Wahid, who was in the army at the time of the Soviet occupation and who was then wooed into the Resistance ranks of Commander Massoud, always said about the Taliban as they made their way south, 'You can't imagine the support they've got from foreign powers. Nobody in Kabul has any idea. They're really powerful. They've got modern means. The government will never hold up against them.'

At the time, we thought he was a pessimist. Now we know he was probably right. But in order to convince myself, I have to go and see these Taliban with my own eyes.

My father wants to go too. We'll take the car. Daoud

will stay with my mother, who's too fragile for this kind of spectacle.

Farad tries to deter us. 'You shouldn't go out,' he tells my father. 'It's not safe. Stay home.'

But we need to witness these incredible events for ourselves. If I were really a reporter, it would be my duty to go to the square. I've never seen Najibullah, except for a few appearances on television, which I don't remember properly because I was too small. Of late, people said that he was writing his autobiography. I was eager to read it. Even traitors, even supporters of the Soviets, are part of our recent history. If you want to be a journalist, you have to read everything, know everything, understand everything.

Soraya and I prudently put on long dresses and our chadors, the veils we normally only wear at home for prayers. My usual gear is jogging trousers, a polo neck or pullover and trainers. But not today. We've been forewarned. Father goes to get the car, which is parked near the mosque, not far from our building. Farad follows us down the stairs, his sturdy made-in-China bicycle on his shoulders. We wait downstairs together for the car to arrive.

One of the neighbours calls out to us, 'Have you heard? It seems they've hung Najibullah on Ariana Square. What do you make of it?'

My father signals discreetly to us to be wary. In Kabul and even in our quarter, which is called Mikrorayan, you never know quite whom you might be talking to. The four modern boroughs that make up this eastern quarter of the capital were built by the Soviets and constitute a kind of concrete village. The great blocks of apartment buildings are numbered block one, block two, and so on in Soviet style. We also have our own commercial centre and school. A lot of high-ranking Afghan Communist Party civil servants lived here, because the area was considered to be more comfortable and luxurious than those with traditional houses. Most of the residents know each other and we, of course, know this neighbour. What we don't know is what banner he might have chosen to shelter himself under this morning.

Soraya answers him politely and with her usual calm sweetness. 'We heard about it, too. We're going to see what's going on.'

'My daughter would love to go with you.'

Farad whispers to Soraya, 'It would be better not to have anyone with us. You never know what might be happening over there.'

Farad has little sisters and a sense of responsibility. And though the neighbour's daughter persists, our 'no' remains a 'no'.

We drive along the road to the main Kabul square. Sitting in the back with Soraya, I think of the wedding we won't be going to. Earlier, when I mourned the dresses we were meant to pick up from the dressmaker's today, my mother reprimanded me harshly. 'Have you got any clue what's going on, Latifa? And here you are talking about dresses!'

My father intervened. 'Don't worry, I'll go and pick them up later.'

I know that I'm a teenager spoiled by her father and pampered by her older sisters. Up until now, I've grown up

9

with a lot of freedom. School, college, the pool on Sundays, shopping expeditions with my friends in pursuit of the latest cassettes and videos, novels to devour late at night in my bed. I pray that the Resistance hasn't let us down.

Father stops on the road. A friend of his, a pharmacist, seeing him at the wheel has signalled to him. The man's brother has an important government post. 'If you're heading towards Ariana Square, I'd turn back right now.'

'We want to see things with our own eyes.'

'All right then. But take care. And stop on your way back. There's something I want to tell you.'

There are fewer people than usual on the streets. We see men, but very few women. The faces I notice are stiff, expressionless. People seem to be in a state of shock. But everything is oddly calm.

It takes us about fifteen minutes to reach the avenue which runs between the airport and Ariana Square. Traffic is congested here. This is the modern centre of the city. My father announces that he's going to circle it once very quickly and then will park further along. We drive in front of the American Embassy, the television headquarters, the Air Ariana building. All the doors are solidly shut.

Tears fill Soraya's eyes. 'Maybe I'll never be able to come and work here again. Even the television centre is closed.'

My father turns at the angle of Peace Avenue where the UN building stands. In front of us is the Ministry of Defence, where Commander Massoud used to have his office. And that's where we see it. Just opposite the Ariana Hotel, Kabul's most luxurious and largely frequented by tourists and western journalists, there's a kind of observation platform used by police to guard the Ministry. Two bodies swing from the improvised gallows. Father tells us to look quickly: he's not intending to go round the square twice.

'Look carefully at their faces. We want to be certain that it really is Najibullah and his brother.'

It really is. They swing side by side, the former president, Najibullah, in traditional Afghan clothes, and his brother in a western suit. One hangs by a plastic pipe passed under his arms, the other by the neck. Najibullah's face is recognizable though blue and covered with great brown and yellow bruises. He must have been lynched before they hung him. His brother's face is intact, but has the pallor of wax. They've shoved cigarettes into Najibullah's mouth, stuffed his pockets with visible banknotes as if to prove his greed. He looks as if he's vomiting cigarettes.

The spectacle is humiliating and so frightening that I burst into tears. I'm both disgusted and afraid. So is my sister. But neither of us can stop staring.

Father parks the car a good distance from the crowd. As he turns off the engine, he says, 'I'm going back there now, but you stay in the car. Don't move. I noticed my friend, the pharmacist. He must have changed his mind and decided to come as well. I'm going to have a word with him.'

We stay alone, huddled against each other and gazing at the little groups that form and disband in the distance.

Farad hasn't exaggerated. The Taliban are wielding whips – or rather, some kind of metallic cable. They hit out at random and with no care for passers-by. They're forcing them to assemble on the square and take in the horrific spectacle. I can't altogether make out the details of their whips. Soraya thinks they have leaded tips. I'm not sure.

'But yes,' she insists. 'Look properly. That one's hitting a boy. Look how he doubles over. An ordinary cable wouldn't hurt that much.'

Ten minutes go by. Alone in the car, hidden beneath our chadors, our heads lowered, we're silent now. We're both thinking of the disaster that has just fallen on our city and we're worrying about what will happen to us. Rumours about the Taliban abound. I fear I won't be going to university. I won't even have the education our mother did. She studied at the senior school in Zarghouna. She didn't wear the veil. Her father had bought her a bicycle, just like mine, so that she could get to school. She grew up at a time when girls wore knee-length skirts. She got a nursing diploma, worked in a hospital, then specialized in gynaecology and got a further degree. Now she's forty-eight, retired and tired out, after having brought up five children and spent most of her life looking after sick women. But two or three times a week, she still sees patients at home and for free.

Our country needs its women. For years now, it's been women who've taken on posts in administration, teaching, health. So many widows, so many children, so much preventative care and emergency work to be done. So many daily battles to be fought against people's ignorance of modern medicine. Mother has lived through so much suffering that the Taliban's arrival in Kabul will take a great toll on her.

Father is on his way back. We can see him in the distance. His shoulders are hunched. He sits down at the wheel without breathing a word. His head is bowed. We respect his silence.

Then, as he starts the engine, he begins to speak.

'I talked with the pharmacist. His brother told him that just before Massoud's troops left the city, one of the Commander's friends came to find Najibullah in the UN building in order to warn him and to propose that he leave the city with them. Najibullah refused. He said he was in the midst of writing his book. He also said that the Taliban would be giving him an important position, maybe even that of prime minister. So he was going to stay.'

In fact many people thought that if the Taliban took power, the king would come back and Najibullah would once again take on some official function. But now, there he is hanging on Ariana Square.

Father is speaking again. 'He stayed on in the UN building without protection. At about four this morning, he saw the head of the Pakistani Secret Service arrive. They had a document that he was to sign instantly. It had been prepared in advance and it signalled his official acceptance of the current Pakistani borders, which gives them all the Peshawar zone that once used to belong to Afghanistan. Najibullah was also asked to give them a list of all the arms and munitions depots that the Soviets had left in Kabul. He didn't want to sign. They beat him and killed him, then hung him on the square. It's his fault if he's died like this. His fault . . . He didn't think the Taliban would dare invade UN headquarters. But they did. God only knows what else they're capable of.'

The information our neighbour has given my father can

be taken on trust. They're good friends. They play chess together and have become intimates. It appears that the pharmacist's brother left Kabul this morning. There was no question of him offering up his arms.

We return to our apartment slowly, taking in everything that's going on in the streets. Women carrying children or dragging them by the hand are heading home briskly after having been to the centre to get news. The city is so quiet that we can hear the echo of their footsteps. A few teenagers have gathered to discuss what they've seen. They gesture dramatically. Najibullah's name is on all lips. When we reach our building, we go up the stairs quickly in fear of possible questions from our neighbours.

Mother sighs with relief as she sees us coming through the door. 'Were you able to see him? Was it really him?'

We tell her everything. She suddenly needs to sit down.

Soraya who has stayed fairly quiet up until now, starts to talk about the Taliban's whips, but Father signals for her to refrain. The doctor has told us to keep Mother as calm as possible. Her nerves won't stand up to any more emotional shocks. Her face is terribly pale beneath her hair, which is already grey and which she wears tied up in back. The look she gives us is full of anguish.

Father goes back out to see his friend, but returns with no news. Neither telephones nor radios work yet. He thinks he'll go out again to get a supply of batteries before night falls. We already have a small stockpile of essentials – rice, which is our daily bread, noodles, oil and flour, in case the bakeries no longer function. My father put down these stores at the beginning of the week when the fighting already showed signs of rising to unprecedented ferocity.

We're used to not having electricity. Electricity is an unstable sprite in Kabul. She comes at precise times for two or three days, then vanishes. So we make do with gas or oil lamps. For cooking and hot water, we use one of those gas-rings fed by a container which holds about ten to fourteen litres. They're easy to get, but cost a fortune. We have a bathroom and taps, but these have long been dry. No plumbing works in our neighbourhood or anywhere else. Ironing is done with an ancient iron we heat on an open fire. While the iron is hot, we lend it to our neighbour. We share and exchange a great deal in Kabul. Nothing that might be useful to someone can be wasted.

At eleven o'clock, we're startled by the sound of the radio. It's been rebaptized Radio Sharia, the name for the rules drawn from the sacred texts of Islam. First there are religious chants. They last for a very long time. Then a man's voice recites a verse from the Koran, before continuing,

The Prophet said to his disciples that their work was to prohibit evil and promote virtue. We have come to reinstate order. From now on, law will be established by the clerics. Preceding governments had no respect for religion. We chased them away and they fled. But all those who participated in the old regime will be safe with us from now on. We ask our brothers to give up all their arms, to deposit them in front of their buildings or at the mosque. And for reasons of security, we ask women not to leave their houses for the time being.

This speech, declaimed with spitfire violence, is followed by religious chants until noon. Then there's silence again. We'll have to wait until the evening to get anything more. Maybe then we'll be lucky enough to hear the BBC or Voice of America's Persian broadcasts.

What to do in the meantime apart from dwell on the worst possible scenarios and rehearse horrible images? We even forget to eat.

There's a knock at the door. It's the building manager come with orders from the Taliban. He alerts my father that he has to go to the neighbouring mosque to deliver up any arms. We don't have any guns, apart from two antiques hanging on the wall.

Father contemplates the old rifle that dates from the twenties and his own grandfather's military service at the time of the war against the British. He hung it carefully up on the wall after his grandfather's death. It's now purely a decorative object. There's a sabre next to it. What could the Taliban do with such arms? I can see from the emotion in my father's gaze that he's unwilling to give up these family treasures. But Mother insists. She begs him to be reasonable.

'To hide anything would be too dangerous . . . in case they search the apartment.'

Sick at heart, Father unhooks the old rifle. It leaves a light trace of its presence on the wall just above a splendid portrait of my mother painted by her brother. She's so beautiful with the black hair of a twenty-year-old girl waving over her shoulders, her vast eyes illuminated by happiness. That beauty has stayed with her, though it has grown a little tarnished with the tests of time.

16

Father unhooks the sabre as well. Silently, he wraps them up. He'll go off alone to deposit these family heirlooms in the mosque with the white flag.

I want to cry. Our family's not one for baring its emotions. We each keep our sorrows to ourselves. Pointless to inflict your own pain on your loved ones, since it will only double theirs. This is a particularly Afghan way of proceeding. It entails a certain dignity and a modesty of emotion in all circumstances. As chattering and expansive as we may be about subjects external to us, we keep silent about our sufferings. The civil war has, I think, increased this dignity and this muteness. We survive with a kind of economy of emotions. It's necessary in order not to go down, or go mad with rage or fear. When my own pain gets too heavy, when I feel it rise up and get close to the point of tumbling over in front of the others, I take refuge in my room and cry savagely, but alone, on my bed.

That Friday, 27 September, heavy with visions of terror, Soraya and I discuss events and what we witnessed over and over. After Chakila's marriage, I had abandoned my single bed to sleep with Soraya. Until now, she'd always told me stories about her trips and the cabin crew or we'd listen to music and she'd make me burst into laughter by holding my nose. That was our way of putting up with the fury of the rocket explosions all around us. My brother, Wahid, had taught us a technique he'd learned at the Front while he was a soldier. In case of violent explosion, you have to open your mouth as wide as possible to prevent any ruptures in the tympanum.

Our girls' room is a refuge marked out by all the little passions of my adolescence. On the wall, there's a poster of the American actress and model Brooke Shields. Soraya has often made me laugh by playing the model: perched on high heels, hands on hips, made up extravagantly, she flounces along an imaginary catwalk and strikes poses. She liked dressing up for me even when I was small, disguising herself in my mother's shoes and dresses.

There's an Elvis poster next to the one of Brooke Shields to show my love of rock music. I have stacks of cassettes. I also have lots of videos of Bollywood films that Daoud goes to fetch for me from my cousin Farad's father who has a video shop we use a lot.

But today, I don't feel like music. Nor can I read. I need to talk. And Soraya is in a worse state than I am. She's even more pessimistic. Her flight assistant's uniform will no longer be able to come out of the wardrobe. She's certain of that. And it suits her wonderfully. Yesterday she came back from Bagram Airport wearing the long white shirt and turquoise trousers that make up Air Ariana's uniform and looking beautiful. Soraya is like our father. She has the blackest hair, cut mid-length, luscious eyes and amazingly thick lashes. Like Chakila, she's always spoiled me. Since I was a baby, she brooded over me, did the housework for me whenever I felt like shirking my duties. Soraya is gentle, rounded, tender, greedy too, but tonight she hasn't swallowed even a mouthful of rice.

We ponder all that we've heard on the BBC about the advance of the Taliban to Kabul, about the massacres in the city of Herat in the spring of 1995. Television showed us pictures of widows, blinded by their burqas, whipped and forced to beg in the streets. As of today, these are no longer distant images, frames on the screen, pictures in the papers. They're an immediate and present reality. They're here.

Yesterday afternoon what was perhaps my last ever walk in freedom took place. My last day as a student . . . I explain to Soraya why I felt impelled to go to Ariana Square.

'I wanted to see Najibullah. I wanted to understand. I was even prepared to be whipped for it . . . to submit, in order to confront the reality we're living. Do you understand, Soraya? I had to persuade myself it was real.'

'That image of the hanged men . . .' my sister echoes. 'It's in my head all the time now, side by side with the sense that everything's over, that the Taliban are more monstrous than I ever imagined. They've given us a symbol to force us to understand that from now on anyone – anyone at all can die at the hand of a Talib. It's all over for us, Latifa, my career is up the spout. I'll never fly again. Did you see the Air Ariana building? They've closed it down, like the television headquarters. No woman will be allowed to work again.'

'Father said that it might be over in a few days, maybe a few weeks. That the Resistance is still active in the north somewhere. The Mujahidin will come back. And I . . . I prefer rocket fire to the Taliban.'

'Father always gives us hope. But I don't believe it this time. Even at the worst moments in the fighting, we never saw anything like this. In 1992, no one tried to hang Najibullah and that's the proof of it. Neither him, nor his brother, even if he was a sad case . . .'

While she was still working in Kabul, my eldest sister, Chakila, told us the sordid tale of Shapour, Najibullah's brother, who had an affair with a young girl. The young girl was called Wida and lived in the first district of Mikrorayan, our very own area. She had met Shapour in the main square and since then, he regularly came to pick her up at school. One day, while her family was away, he saw her all the way back to her parents' apartment. I don't know who urged the other to go up into the empty flat, but everyone surmises they did go up. Because alas, Wida got pregnant. Her lover should have married her. But despite her insistence, he refused. And so, Wida invited him home one day for a last talk, and when he still refused, she took his gun and committed suicide. At the beginning, no one dared point any fingers. Then the rumour started making the rounds that Shapour was certainly responsible for her death. Wida's parents fled into exile. They were frightened. To be Najibullah's brother at that time was to be beyond blame, untouchable.

'Whatever his crimes were,' Soraya says, 'the manner of his death was barbaric. These people can't be Afghans. Remember I told you when I came back from Dubai on Wednesday, that there were supposed Afghans on the plane that touched down after us. The hostess told me they'd been expelled from the Emirates because they had no passports or because their visas had expired, something like that. In any case, my colleague was struck by their behaviour. They were extremely contemptuous of the female staff. I wonder now whether perhaps they hadn't come to help the Taliban.'

20

In Kabul we always have to ask ourselves who's who and if they really are who they say they are. The first rule of security is never to share speculations or opinions with anyone outside the family. Our principle is to remain as neutral as the situation permits. Only one thing unites Afghans across the complexity of their ethnic divides and that's the rejection of any occupying foreign force – whether they be British, Pakistani, Arab or, of course, Soviet.

The Afghanis rose up against the Russians, organizing a Resistance as best they could. The Mujahidins' war against the Soviets lasted ten bloody years and was fought out against a rhythm of interchangeable puppet regimes installed by Moscow.

After the Russians went, the resisters set up in Kabul under the leadership of Commander Massoud in 1992. Our lives were now lived to a new battle rhythm, since all the other war lords now fought against Massoud, the Tajik. Foremost amongst them was his old Pashtun enemy, the terrible Gulbuddin Hekmatyar, chief of the Hezb-e-Islami, the most extreme fundamentalist party and supported by Pakistan. But even those years didn't put an end to the battle-story. Now we've walked into a new era, under the lashes of the Taliban whip. And in all my short life, this feels like the most terrible day.

Soraya is crying. She's never really seen war up close like this. The last time that Hekmatyar pounded the city with rockets, 1 January 1994, she was on a flight to Dubai. Kabul Airport had already been destroyed and Air Ariana's planes were forced to use the Bagram landing field, forty kilometres away from the capital. It was impossible to land here in the middle of battle. So Soraya's pilot landed in New Delhi instead. Soraya was effectively stuck there for six months. She spent her time in a hotel room alone or watching television with her colleagues.

On the day of Chakila's wedding, two years ago, over 300 rockets fell on Kabul while we were in the midst of the marriage feast. I remember the proverb we recited as a family to console each other: joy and sadness are sisters.

Just after the wedding, my brother Wahid went off to India, before finally settling in Moscow. While he was still at home, my great love for him was accompanied by an indefinable fear. Strict about the observation of religious rules, he was the first to give us the chadors we're wearing today.

'Do you remember,' I ask Soraya, 'the day Wahid brought us these chadors? We thought they were far, far too big.'

'I told him we'd cut them in two.'

Our father didn't agree with my elder brother's wish to regulate our clothes. He didn't want us to be any different from the other girls at school. For us, the chador is reserved for prayer in our private quarters, in the intimacy of our rooms. We never wear the chador in the street. Nor does our mother. But for love of my brother, I was prepared to obey him. He gave us sermons on the length of our skirts, on the rather modest décolleté of our T-shirts in summer. Chakila and Soraya let him go on, or at worse, rebuked him briskly. 'I'm quite big enough to know how to dress myself, thank you' or 'Mind your own business.'

My parents worried about the influence of fundamentalism on his character and they advised him that after all the military service he had done and war he had witnessed, it would be a good idea for him to go and live in a peaceful country.

I wonder what he's doing now and whether he'll get married one day. Lots of wives have been proposed for him, but he's refused them. The army isn't compatible with family life. Mother prefers that he lives far away and that he participates in no more of the battles from which he's already suffered too much and which have hardened him terribly.

Daoud doesn't know quite what to do with himself. Protected by the whole family and by his older and admired brother who told him 'one in the family is enough', he kept away from the army. Will he need to hide now in order to be able to work? At the end of his economics studies, he could only find a job as a ticket seller at Air Ariana.

They say that the Taliban enlists young Afghans by force in the provinces; that they send them to the Front to burn down houses and destroy villages.

In the afternoon, Daoud prefers to go out instead of my father in order to stock up on the batteries we'll need if we're to enter a state of siege. He's not the only one set on that mission. When he comes back in the evening, he tells us that he met lots of people doing the same thing. Mother didn't want him to go out. I heard her arguing with him not to take the risk . . .

'And if they nab you? If they imprison you like the Communists did your brother? Or if they force you to kill?'

My poor father has the entire weight of the family on his shoulders. He fears for Mother's heath. He worries that the Taliban will take away his son and that his daughters will be condemned to a cloistered life, with no hope of any career. On top of all that, he has no idea what state his textile warehouse may be in: it's situated on the road the Taliban took as they fought their way into the city.

My father already lost everything once in 1991 at the time of General Tanai's failed coup d'état. Rockets then completely destroyed his shop on the busy Jade Maywan Avenue. Everything went up in smoke. Business was good in that shop. Father made a fair living. He imported textiles from Japan and the Soviet Union. Without being rich, we weren't poor either. The day the shop went up, so did the greatest part of his assets.

After many difficulties, he set up again only to have to submit to a second disaster in 1993, at the time of Hekmatyar's assault on Kabul. My father's warehouse was on the Pole Mahmoud Khan, right in the midst of the combat zone where the ground was truffled with anti-personnel mines. He couldn't go anywhere near it. The television showed us pictures of smoking ruins. Three months went by before he could finally make his way to the area. Amidst the rubble of shells and explosives, there was nothing left. He went to the hospital where one of his former security guards lay. He had barely survived and he told my father a hellish story. When this poor man had tried to convince the warriors not to burn down the warehouse with their flame-throwers, they shot at him. They even shot at the dogs. Seriously wounded, the guard played dead until a government tank went past at the end of the day and picked him up.

Why burn warehouses full of merchandise? Why kill civilians and even dogs? Hekmatyar's troops were barbaric and determined to conquer Massoud and take back Kabul.

What it meant for my father was that once more he had to start from zero, this time with the help of government loans for merchants struck by disaster. He managed to build up his business again and even to pay back a large part of his debt. He thought he was on top of things. But since yesterday's incursions, nothing is less certain. If there's a third catastrophe, I don't know how he'll manage to make good his financial situation.

That evening we finally manage to tune into the BBC. Our ears are glued to the low volume of the radio. We don't want to alert our neighbours.

The journalist has little news to announce that we don't already know. He describes the battles in the periphery of Kabul, where the government forces of Commander Massoud fought and were defeated by the Taliban.

We already know that the battle is no longer on the outskirts, but right here in our city, in the centre of our lives. And that tonight, we'll have to try to sleep with the nightmare of that reality.

2

Canary in a Cage

On the wall of our room Soraya has pinned a postcard of a magnificent rose, purple on a blue base. I've been staring at it obstinately ever since she got up to make breakfast.

Dawn on this Saturday, 28 September 1996, brings with it a taste of annihilation. Yesterday, the neighbours were agitated. There were voices in the hall discussing whether any telephone lines might yet be working, wondering if news might yet be had of the rest of their respective families. Today all I hear is a thick silence. My father won't go out to run this morning. The Taliban are sure to disapprove of jogging and we have other preoccupations. The banks were closed yesterday, as they always are on Friday, but Father has to go to the bank this morning to try and draw out money for the days to come.

Mother is still asleep, knocked out by her pills. Nor is there any music yet from Daoud's room. In order not to wake her, he must be whispering with Soraya in the kitchen. They won't be going to work this morning and I won't be going to my courses.

A sense of intense fatigue overtakes me like a sadness weighing down all of my body, yet leaving my eyes dry. I can't get up. Instead I'm taking a trip round my sister's postcard collection. A red tulip, an unknown white flower that comes from New Delhi . . . Soraya adds to her paper garden with every trip. In Kabul itself, there have been no flowers for a long time – apart from the plastic bouquets imported from Taiwan.

What next? I've already said my prayers on the rug my father brought back from Mecca. I'll read the last article my friend, Saber, gave me for our homemade magazine. A group of us have been working on it for about two years now. We produce one copy of each issue. It makes the rounds of the neighbourhood, passed from hand to hand, and eventually comes back to me, suitably dog-eared. The last issue's in my wardrobe; the new one is just being prepared. But what's the use now of writing articles and finding photos about Madonna, or poetry, or the latest fashion or Indian film? If the Taliban take control of the media, there'll be nothing left to read in the papers. They'll be fully Islamicised or will cease to exist.

Thursday morning, I did part of my entrance exam for the journalism faculty. That very evening, when Saber and his sister, Farida, expressed worries about whether I was revising enough for my final which would take place that winter, I shrugged my shoulders and said, 'Easy peasy.'

'What was the special subject in the exam?'

'We had to choose a piece of news and prepare it for three different media – newspapers, radio and television.

'What did you choose?'

'A true story, even though I don't altogether remember the source: "Mr Bin Laden, Saudi friend of the Taliban, proposes to finance the construction of mosques in Afghanistan."'

I'd heard this on the radio, I no longer know exactly when, but it had struck me. Though I knew almost nothing about this Bin Laden, except perhaps that as a Saudi he must have a lot of money. I'd got a good grade for my first attempt.

Before they left, Saber returned a book I'd loaned them, *A Red Flower For Your Sorrow* by the Iranian writer, Parwiz Ghasi Said. A sad love story which all of us young people were reading at the moment and which I had adored.

'So what did you think of it?'

Saber made a face in order not to look moved, though I know he's in love with a girl in the neighbourhood. He tells me everything and I tell everything to his sister. I also know that his parents think Saber is much too young to enter any engagement negotiations with the girl's family.

I force myself to think of living things, futile things, like my dress for example, which is waiting for me at the dressmaker's and which Father has promised to fetch soon, despite Mother's reproving eye. She thinks he caters too much to my whims. I adore my father and he gives me more or less everything I want. Even Daoud, when he was a student, used me as an intermediary when he wanted to ask something of Father. Every time I want some money to buy a cassette or nail polish, Mother reproaches me. 'Think of the family budget, Latifa. Don't overdo things.'

Yesterday she was altogether outraged that I was still thinking of the wedding on a day like that. But I couldn't help it. I hadn't even seen the dress finished . . . I know I'm being superficial, but I'm struggling to live the normal life of a girl my age. It's a way of putting off the inevitable imprisonment that awaits me. That awaits all us girls and women.

I can always carry on lying here in contemplation of this postcard rose. It's like an obsessive idea, like a weight on my forehead: I won't be able to go to university. I did that exam for nothing. I'll stay trapped in the house without a goal and without a future project. For how long? Weeks, months will go by before the Resistance will be able to chuck out these rapacious clerics. Years maybe. No one knows where Commander Massoud and his men have taken refuge. They were beaten back, Radio Sharia announced, and we won't know any more than that for a long time.

Breakfast is gloomy. Radio Sharia is nothing like Radio Kabul. There is no news. The programme will only begin as it did yesterday at eleven o'clock with religious music and the prohibitions of mullahs.

I hate this morning, devoid of any sense. Before this it was a pleasure to eat hot bread and drink sweetened tea while listening to the *Payam Sobhgahan* programme on Radio Kabul: news, Persian poetry, music. At about eight, Daoud and Soraya would leave for work and I would go to my classes. Only my mother stayed home with Bingo for company. On some days, she would do her free consultations with the women of the neighbourhood whose husbands were too strict to allow them to go to hospital where they would be under the care of men. This is the reason most doctors in Kabul are women, especially in gynaecology.

While waiting for Radio Sharia to honour us with the orders of the new regime, we can only listen, between eight and nine, to religious music, a reading of some verses from the Koran and prayers. Daoud will turn the radio on every hour again, just in case there's something new.

I go back to my room while Soraya does the dishes. Father is going to take a careful stroll round the neighbourhood in order to run some errands, go to the bank, and try to learn something of what's happening from the whispers of friends. Mother stretches out on the living room sofa. She's already falling asleep again, her gaze wan. She didn't even grumble at me when Soraya did the dishes in my place. She doesn't seem to be interested in anything this morning.

When Father comes back, the news is bad. The banks are still shut, as are the shops and all administrative buildings. Only the Ministries of Defence and the Interior are functioning. He's seen broken televisions scattered haphazardly in the streets like rubbish, cassette tapes stripped out and hanging from trees, turning slowly in the autumn wind like sinister garlands. The streets are full of dejected people. The queues in front of shops grow longer and longer.

He's now going to the mosque to turn over his family's antique weapons that are wrapped in a rag. My poor father, so solid, so stout, so respectable. What humiliation for him. He hasn't shaved this morning and his face is grey and sad. The sprouting beard makes him look ill.

Eleven o'clock. Radio Sharia is back in action to announce that the Prime Minister of the Interim Government composed of six mullahs has decreed the following:

Henceforth, the country will be run strictly according to Islamic law. All foreign ambassadors' posts are hereby suspended. The new decrees according to Sharia Law are:

Any person in possession of a firearm must deposit
   this at a military post or at the nearest mosque;
Girls and women are not allowed to work outside
   the home;
All women who have to leave their houses must be
   accompanied by a mahram;
Public transport will be segregated, with a bus for
   women and a separate bus for men;
According to Sharia law men must grow their beards
   and cut their moustaches;
Men must wear a turban or white beret on their
   heads;
Suits and ties are forbidden. Traditional Afghani
   dress must be worn;
Women and girls must wear the burqa;
Women and girls are forbidden to wear brightly
   coloured clothes beneath their burqa;
Nail polish, lipstick and make-up are forbidden;
All Muslims must say their prayers at the specified
   times and in the place they find themselves.

On the following days a torrent of decrees pours out of Radio Sharia, all in the same threatening voice, all in the name of the Sharia law.

Displaying photos of animals or humans is
forbidden;

A woman cannot take a taxi unless she is accompanied by a mahram;

No male doctor is permitted to touch the body of a
woman under the pretext of a consultation;

A woman may not go to a men's tailor;

A young woman must not engage in conversation
with a young man. If they do so, they must be
married immediately after this breach;

Muslim families may not listen to music, even
during a wedding ceremony;

Families are prohibited from taking photos or
making videos, even during a marriage;

Engaged women may not go to a beauty salon, even
during the preparations for a marriage;

It is forbidden for non-Muslim names to be given
to babies;

All non-Muslims, that is Hindus and Jews, must
wear yellow garments or some yellow cloth. Their
houses must bear a yellow flag so that they are
recognizable;

No merchant may sell alcohol;

No merchant is permitted to sell women's under-
garments;

When the police are punishing an offender, no one
has the right to question or criticize their actions;

All offenders against the decrees of the Sharia Law
will be punished on the public square.

This time they're really murdering us – girls and women. They're killing us in silence and with cunning. The worst prohibitions, already applied in the greatest part of our country, annihilate us by marginalizing us from society. All women are implicated in this, from the youngest to the oldest. No more work for women means the total disintegration of the medical services and the administration. No more school for girls, no more health care for women, and no fresh air to be breathed anywhere. Back to the home, women! Or bury yourselves beneath your burqa. Far from the eyes of men. All this means a total negation of individual liberty – a stunning sexual racism.

The ultimate insult to Afghans, men and women alike, is that a new ministry has been created. It has a ridiculous name: Ministry for the Repression of Vice and the Promotion of Virtue – AMR Bel Mahrouf in Afghani.

I take refuge in my room and stare at my possessions – my books, clothes, photos, comics, music, videos, posters. And yes, my nail polish and Soraya's lipstick. There is nothing to be done but to pack up all this in cartons and somehow hide it in the cupboard. I'm prostrate and raging by turns, weeping the second after. This personal inventory feels intolerable to each of the three women in my family.

Despite her state, my mother has started to pack up her prohibited objects personally – the family photos of births and weddings, her own and Chakila's. She has taken down the magnificent portrait of herself painted by her brother. It's a picture that depicts a woman in the full bloom of her powers. Her exposed face is intolerable to the Taliban.

While we store our girlhood treasures in the wardrobe,

my mother disguises her own souvenirs of her student days, of her youth, of her early days as a wife and mother, and hides them at the back of a kitchen cupboard. I put all my best dresses in a suitcase, only keeping out my trousers and black trainers. Soraya does the same thing. Her beautiful hostess' uniform, her short and brightly-coloured skirts, her blouses, jumpers and high heels have all grown indecent overnight. When she's finished she goes to help Mother inspect the apartment for any other prohibited materials we may have omitted: calendars, football posters, the music in Daoud's room.

Tears overwhelm me when I'm back in the middle of our room, alone, amidst the remaining books that still need to be packed. I feel dizzy. While I kept myself busy, I was fooling myself with the notion that I was simply packing up for a brief move. Now I can't pretend any more. My eye falls on a cartoon I cut out of a paper last year. Two scientists are bent over a microscope, watching some Taliban squirming on a slide. The scientists look perplexed. In the caption they ask each other what exactly are these strange bacteria they've just discovered.

Horrible bacteria, I think. Dangerous and virulent because they propagate by spreading a serious disease, one that strikes a mortal blow at the freedom of half of humanity. It's simple to propagate this disease. All it takes is for the Taliban to declare – with the backing of brute force – that they're the indisputable masters of the Sharia, the rules laid down in the Koran. In fact, they twist these for their own use, paying no respect to the sacred book. Our family is a religious one: my father and mother both know what Sharia means to a good Muslim. And the recommendations of the Sharia have nothing to do with what we've just had imposed on us.

The Taliban have already prohibited pictures of animals. Soon they'll prohibit the living dogs and birds. I'm certain of that. On our living room terrace (which Father has transformed into a glazed conservatory in order to protect us from malicious and snooping eyes) we have a canary in a cage. The canary whistles beautifully at daybreak.

When Father comes back from the mosque, he finds me in tears in my room.

'Take it easy, Latifa. No one knows yet how things will turn out. We have to be patient. None of this will last, you'll see.'

'Father, we have to let the canary go. I want him to be free. At least let him be free.'

Opening the cage feels like a necessary act – an important symbol. I watch the canary hesitate in front of his unknown freedom. Then he flies off with a flap of wings and disappears into the cloudy autumn sky. He's taking my freedom with him. I hope both of them find shelter in some serene valley.

Everything has changed. The world has turned upside down. My father continues to get up for morning prayers, but he can no longer go jogging because the Taliban refuse to allow anyone, but themselves, to run in the streets. Soraya, Daoud and I get up around nine or ten. We're already tired, despite the lateness. We have no desires. My father and brother have been forced to grow beards. We all feel we look dirty, tired, sad. No one turns the radio on any more, because there's no news, no music, no poetry. Only propaganda. And decrees.

Whistling kettles are prohibited.

Dogs and birds are prohibited.

I was right. Our canary is already far away. We and no one else decided on his freedom. But now, we have to separate ourselves from Bingo, our white Afghan, whose coat is so thick he looks like a little bear. Bingo has always been with me. My first memory of him goes back to a colour photo in the album my mother has hidden in the kitchen. I'm about five and wearing a kilt, a red polo neck and a straw hat. Bingo stands on his hind legs, leaning against me, his paws in my hands. His long muzzle pointing towards my eldest sister, Chakila, he seems to be saying, 'Save me. I'm meant to run on all four legs.'

It's altogether impossible for us to abandon Bingo in the street, like some dog-owners have done with their pets. Father takes Bingo to my uncle's instead. He has a house with a garden. Bingo, the dissident four-legged Afghan can hide in the house during the day and go out for an airing at night. I know he'll be well looked after there.

Our father has lost his business again. He couldn't get close to the area where his warehouse is until some three weeks after the arrival of the Taliban. There were mines everywhere. He kept his distance, but he could see that the years of hard work had been transformed into rubble.

He doesn't complain, in order not to overwhelm Mother with yet another intractable problem. He's going to try and work something out with a Pakistani associate, invest what he's got left in a new enterprise in the hope that it will provide some revenue. But it will be complicated. It won't provide him with a daily occupation and he'll miss that. From now on, he too will be something of a prisoner in our apartment – one who has to do the shopping and cooking, which he doesn't mind at all. He's always cooked, especially in the days when Mother worked regularly at the hospital.

His beard has grown long enough now for us to tease him about his new look from time to time or about the desirable length of a Taliban special. He takes our ribbing with a mixture of cool and contempt. 'My beard belongs to the Taliban and not to me,' he says.

For his part, Daoud has already learned how he and his friends can get hold of video cassettes. They come from Pakistan through black market circuits that are hardly new. On top of that my uncle still has some in his shop. It's a curious paradox: we're forbidden to buy tape recorders, television sets, audio or video cassettes, yet many of the shops still have them amongst their goods. Nobody buys any of this officially. They just somehow get hold of it. It seems that the Taliban hypocritically allow some underground trade to go on, because if it stopped, all Kabul's shops would go under.

Home life now runs to the rhythm of Father and Daoud's exits and entrances. They bring all the news from the outside world – from the bazaar, the greengrocer, the shopping centre or the mosque. We listen to them eagerly.

'Afghans are disgusted with the Taliban version of our

religion with all their ridiculous laws. We've always been Muslim and no one recognizes himself in their Islam. They force people to stop any old place on the street to say their prayers. A man told me he'd been stopped five times and each time he had to kneel. People are also saying that at the mosque, at the moment when you're meant to put your dearest wish to God, a lot of men are praying, "Dear God, please suppress the Taliban." Whenever they force us to pray, the prayer turns against them . . .'

The days are interminable dark tunnels of nothingness. I spend most of my time stretched out in my room reading or looking at the ceiling. No more running or cycling, no more English classes or newspapers. My body grows progressively softer as does my brain, helped along by an overdose of rosy Indian films that Daoud brings me. So that the Taliban can't see the flickering light of the screen, my uncle came over and painted most of our windows black. The little living room, the dining room that looks onto the street, as well as the terrace and bedrooms, are all blackened now. Only the kitchen window on the opposite side remains unpainted. From it we can see the mosque and the school, where now only the boys are left sitting round the mullah who's reciting the Koran.

My head is empty of projects. Sometimes I pace round the apartment like a prisoner round his cell. I go and sit on the sofa or the bench or a rug. Then I walk along the hall that leads to the kitchen and back to my room again. I sit, lie down, study the pattern of the rugs in ever greater detail, return to the television, lie down again. Never have I looked at the furniture or the objects in our house with

such attention. A crumb of bread on the table catches my
interest; a bird in the sky fascinates me. Mother is distant
and laid low; she's not interested in what Soraya and I are
doing any more, as we don't do anything.

From time to time, Saber comes to visit me. Occasionally
Mother sees a burqa-clad patient. They come from the
neighbourhood and are always in a hurry, always anxious.
I open the door to them and they disappear into the living
room with Mother. Their husbands wait downstairs, outside
the building.

One day at the end of winter, I open the door to a
woman in a burqa and think that she's one of my mother's
clandestine patients. But she starts asking me bizarre questions.

'You're Latifa, aren't you? Alia's daughter? Saber's friend?'
Without quite understanding what she wants, I make to
close the door again, but she insists on coming in. 'Yes,
yes, it really is you.'

Suddenly she bursts out laughing and lifts up her burqa.
It's only then that I recognize Saber's sister.

'Farida, it's you! You frightened me. What are you doing
in this get-up?'

'My elder sister came to visit and I made fun of her. But
now, I've come to make fun of you. Because I'm going to
make use of this to get around in, to go out. Go on, try
it on.'

It's a shock for me to see Farida dressed like this. Of
course, I've seen burqas worn before the Taliban occupied
our city. Some country women who came to consult my
mother wore them by custom and choice. They were,

however, a fairly rare sight in Kabul. On the other hand, it's clear that the burqa was quite useful during the civil war for women who served as secret messengers and information bearers. Those indistinguishable faces and anonymous female forms sometimes hid resisters in trousers, too.

When we met these voluminously robed figures in the street, my school friends and I would giggle. We nicknamed them 'bottles' or 'upside down cauliflowers' or 'storage sacks'. When there were several of them, we called them a regiment of parachutists. A stupid joke made us hoot with laughter. It's the story of a Japanese man who comes home after a trip to Afghanistan and he tells his friends that over there, men are way ahead of the Japanese and have really got things sorted. 'Why?' his friends ask and he says, 'Because they walk around in the streets holding a large bottle by the hand!'

I look at this garment, its woven cloth flowing all the way down to the ground from a closely fitted bonnet which completely covers the head. Some of these burqas are shorter and easier to wear. But what really frightens me is the little bit of embroidered latticework around the eyes and the nose.

'My father bought us some, but not quite so long.'

'My sister found this one at an aunt's house. It's old. And my aunt was tall. Try it on. If you want to go out one day, you'll need to be completely covered.'

I do what she asks in order to please her, but also to see what it feels like being in there. It's suffocating. The cloth sticks to my nose. I have a lot of trouble adjusting the embroidered lattice slits in front of my eyes.

'So? Can you see me?' Farida asks.

I see her as long as I stand directly in front of her. In order to turn my head, I have to keep some of the cloth clutched beneath my chin so that the eye holes stay in place. In order to look behind me, I have to turn round completely. I can feel the rustle of my own breath inside the garment. I'm hot. My feet get tangled up in the material. I'll never be able to wear this. I now understand the stiff robot-like walk of the 'bottle women', their unflinching look directly in front of them or fixed rigidly on any unsuspected obstacle. I now know why they hesitate for so long before crossing the street, why it takes them an eternity to walk upstairs. These phantoms that now roam the streets of Kabul have a terrible time avoiding bicycles, buses and carts. It's even worse trying to run away from the Taliban. This is not a garment. It's a moving prison.

But if I want to leave the house, I have no choice but to hide inside one. It's that or disguising myself as a boy, cutting my hair and getting a beard to grow. So there's no real choice. For the moment, I don't feel up to it. The grill-work slits at the eyes of the burqa remind me of a canary's cage. And the canary, this time, is me.

I climb out of the burqa feeling humiliated and furious. My face belongs to me. The Koran says that a woman can be veiled, but that she must remain recognizable. The Taliban want to steal my face, forbid us all our faces. That's out of the question. I won't allow it. I won't give in. I won't go out with Farida.

'You can't stay in here all your life.'

'I'm frightened. That's all. Frightened of tripping up

41

inside it, of getting myself noticed. Frightened of being beaten in the street, because I've allowed a centimetre of myself to show or because I've somehow lifted the thing in order to sneeze. If I had to run in order to get away, I'd never manage.'

'OK. So this burqa's too long for you. Get a shorter one.'

'No. Everyone says they're kidnapping young women in order to marry them forcibly to some Taliban or other.'

'Well, I want to go out. My brother's going to accompany me. You're not at risk if your brother's with you. Ask Daoud to take you out.'

I shake my head definitively. I won't go. Besides I have no wish to see rows of women scraping the walls out of fear, hiding as they walk. It'll make me even more depressed when I get home. If I get home . . .

The programmes on Radio Sharia are always the same: from eight to nine there's the reading of the Koran and prayers; from nine to ten thirty there are propaganda texts, the pronouncement of new decrees, some of which are sung as an Arabic litany as if that would make us believe they really do come from the Koran. This is followed by an interruption in the service until six o'clock in the evening, when we have the so-called 'death notices' of Taliban heroes. After that, there's the news, which is always identical and always celebrates the advances of the Taliban, without ever uttering a word, needless to say, about any combat with the Resistance or about any villages which can't or haven't been taken. Finally at nine thirty, after the reading of a few sacred texts, Radio Sharia shuts up shop.

At midday, one or other of us proposes, without much conviction, that we should perhaps make something to eat . . . The apartment resembles a prison or a hospital. Silence weighs heavily on all of us. As none of us do much, we haven't got much to tell each other. Incapable of sharing our emotions, we each enclose ourselves in our own fear and distress. Since everyone is in the same black pit, there isn't much point in repeating time and again that we can't see clearly.

I drag myself about. I don't bother getting dressed any more. Sometimes I go for three or four days without changing my clothes, day or night. The neighbours' telephone no longer rings. It's cut off. On the day when the line is re-established, my father hesitates to use it; we know the Taliban listen to everything, watch everything.

Sometimes Daoud's friends come over to watch films secretly. Farida and Saber drop round from time to time to pay me a visit. They're more adventurous than we are. They leave their house. I can't seem to face it. I feel as if the only form of resistance left to us is to stay locked up and not have to see them.

Only at the beginning of 1997, some four months after the arrival of the Taliban, does Farida finally convince me to risk the streets of Kabul with her. The pretext is that we'll fetch the last issue of our magazine from our friend Maryam's house. She had asked for it a little while back.

I really can't see the necessity of going, but Farida insists. 'You have to get out,' she says. 'You look terrible, unwell, and there's no better way of confronting reality. If you stay locked up in here any longer, you'll go mad.'

I disappear beneath my burqa and in the company of Farida and Saber, we begin our bizarre 'walk'. I haven't left the house for four months. I feel oddly like a convalescent, lost and too fragile for the escapade. The street looks huge, too big, and I feel I'm constantly being stared at, watched by invisible eyes. In order not to draw attention to ourselves, we only whisper beneath our burqas. Saber is always at our side, closer than a shadow.

The route takes us past our old senior school. Taliban are guarding the entrance. On the neighbouring sports ground, the trees wear their strange garlands of cassette tapes. They've also tied them to the baskets we use to store our trainers, and to the volleyball net. My father had mentioned this to me, but I thought it was only a provisional demonstration of the Taliban's disapproval of our 'western' tastes. It turns out that the tapes are systematically rehung, banners of what is forbidden. No images. No music.

A little further along the road we see four women in burqas walking in our direction. Suddenly a Taliban pickup van appears from nowhere and brakes in front of them with a hellish noise. Taliban leap out, brandishing their cable-whips and, without a word, without any explanation, they start whipping the women despite the fact that they're completely hidden behind their burqas and couldn't be more modest. The women scream, but no one comes to their aid. Then, they start to run away, clumsy in their heavy garb, but the Taliban pursue them, lashing out without cease. I see blood dripping from the women's shoes.

Petrified, unable to move, I feel I've literally been turned to stone. They're going to come towards me now. I know it. Farida takes my arm and shakes me brutally.

'Run. We have to run. Come on.'

With one hand, I hold the burqa to my face, with the other Farida. We run like lunatics, run until we have no more breath. Saber stays behind us, a laughable form of protection; he knows he couldn't possibly stop the Taliban. But he's there, nonetheless. While we run, I have no idea whether the Taliban are chasing us. I think I feel them at my back and that at any moment their lashing whips will encircle me and I'll topple over.

Luckily we're not far from home and the stairs of our building swallow us up in under five minutes. Once on the threshold, I can neither speak nor breathe. I'm sobbing, out of control. Farida catches her breath and mumbles I don't know what, though it sounds like curses against the Taliban. She's far more of a rebel than I am.

Saber, who's right behind us, understands what happened and explains to his sister. 'They whipped them because they were wearing white shoes . . .'

'What do you mean, white shoes? Are they forbidden as part of the latest decree?'

'It's the colour of the Taliban flag. Women aren't allowed to wear white. It means they're trampling the flag.'

Decrees follow upon decrees with no rhyme or reason. To me, however, they seem to bear an insidious and certain logic: the extermination of Afghani women.

A woman went out one day covered only with her burqa. She held the Koran pressed tightly to her bosom. The Taliban whipped her. She protested, 'You haven't the right.

Look at what's written in the Koran!' Alas, in the ensuing commotion, her Koran fell to the ground and none of her attackers stooped to pick it up . . . Yet it's known that the Koran must never be placed directly on the ground. If they had really read it, the Taliban would have known. But they pay little heed to the traditional principles of our religion. Their decrees are aberrations that spin off from the sacred text. The Koran notably states that there are two occasions on which a woman can show her intimate parts to a man – when she's with her husband or when she's with a doctor. Preventing women from being treated by a male doctor at the same time as preventing them from working in the medical professions, shows a clear desire to destroy them.

The profound depression that is gradually swallowing up my mother is an example both of the suffering women endure and the Taliban's utter negation of them. My mother used to be a spontaneous woman, a free spirit. She always felt at home in her family, her studies and her work. Even her marriage was not an arranged one. When she went to university, she wore skirts or trousers. During the sixties, she'd go to the Zainab cinema and even take her sisters with her. During that time, the women of Kabul claimed their rights. In 1975, the United Nations Year of Women, President Daoud's government democratically decreed that 'the Afghan woman, like the Afghan man, has the right to control her own body, to choose her career and her husband.'

A feminist association worked against the odds to apply this law in the provinces and in the most remote parts of the country. Militants struggled against the deeply rooted traditions of various tribes. Mother told me that in certain parts of the countryside, disobedient children would be disciplined with the threat that an 'unveiled woman' would be sent for, a veritable ogress. 'If you don't behave,' they were told, 'she'll devour you.'

Mother did her nurse's training at the Mastourat Hospital in Kabul, a women's institution. There, she worked with eminent professors – Dr Fatahe Najm, Dr Nour Ahman Balaiz and Dr Kerramuddin. She was part of the team that tended to King Zaher's mother. During the Soviet period, she worked in the crèche in our neighbourhood, which had the added benefit of a place for me during her work hours. One day, when I was four, she rushed me out of the crèche. She was furious as she bundled me into a taxi, dropped me at home and hurried off again. Many years later, she told me the reason behind her anger and haste. She had brusquely reproached a Soviet nurse who was vaccinating the children and using the same syringe for all of them, thereby risking general contamination. It was 1984 and my mother was well aware of the dangers of this kind of practice.

Called in by the administration of the crèche that very day, she was disciplined in no uncertain terms.

'You have no right to argue with the procedures undertaken by a Soviet nurse.'

'Even if there's professional misconduct? You know what's at stake here?'

'The Soviets are in charge. It's none of your business what they do. You'll apologize to the nurse. Otherwise, I shall be forced to consider you a counter-revolutionary.'

'The woman committed a serious offence. She endangered the lives of Afghan children. As an Afghan woman, I can't possibly apologize to her. I'm sorry.'

'You give me no choice but to fire you then.'

Mother attempted to get her professional file back from the Ministry of Health, but oddly, it had disappeared. Minister Nabi Kamyar, in an attempt to quieten things down, offered my mother the possibility of enrolling in a competitive examination which would lead to the specialist training of her choice. Mother did well and the following year she was sent to Prague for a six-month specialization in gynaecology. She got the best grades in her year. When she came back to Kabul, she went straight to the Ministry.

'I thank you for organizing this training for me. And now I'm going to retire. I can't work under the orders of the Soviets.'

The minister managed to convince her that she should come and work with him in the Ministry of Health, before ultimately retiring – which she did three years later, but only in order to continue practising from home. Until the arrival of the Taliban, that is.

This so-called retirement was hardly a way of turning herself into a homebody who cooked and raised her youngest daughter. Mother has never been a fanatic when it comes to housekeeping. And my father was quite happy with her ways. He even hired a cook at one point to allow her more time to pursue her career.

Not working suits Mother even less well than it suits her daughters. Soraya and I are young. All hope is not lost, as Father keeps telling us. But for his wife, whom he sees retreating more deeply, day by day, into a forced retirement, he fears the worst.

When Father goes out or friends come to visit, they only recount abominable, revolting, nightmare scenes. How is one to accommodate the fact that a woman has had her fingers cut off in bright daylight by the religious police, simply because she was wearing nail polish? Father tries to shelter Mother from the most violent of these narratives.

But you don't really need to go out to confront the horror we're living.

At the beginning of the winter of 1997, we heard a woman screaming in the street, 'My son is innocent. My son is innocent.'

Through the window, I recognized the Mother of Aimal, a young boy who lives in the neighbouring block. Three Taliban were savaging him with the butts of their Kalashnikovs. They hit him methodically, and particularly on the ribs. Soraya and I pulled back quickly so as not to be seen, but the boy's cries cut us to the quick.

Then came the silence. The Taliban had gone. Downstairs there was only Aimal's weeping mother, bent over the inanimate body of her son. When the doctors came to take him to the hospital, it was already too late. Aimal had been dead for an hour.

Daoud learned what had happened. Aimal had invited some friends, all between fifteen and seventeen, to watch a film on his video, despite the prohibitions in place. The Taliban raided the apartment and caught the band of six youths in the act. They destroyed the television and the video player, tore the tape out of the cassette, before marching the boys outside. There, they asked to whom the material belonged and Aimal admitted it was his. As punishment, they insisted that the boys hit each other, an act which Afghans find supremely humiliating, even for young boys. Aimal didn't hit hard enough and one of the Taliban approached him.

'I'll show you how it's done.'

So he set upon him, first with his fists, then with his rifle. Aimal's mother tried to interpose herself, but one of the Taliban hit her so hard she went flying against barbed wire. Then, like a lynch mob, they all joined in beating the youth with the butts of their rifles.

When the Taliban entered Kabul, Aimal's family were amongst those who threw flowers from their windows to salute their victory. Since this tragedy, his mother spends all her time apologising to everyone for having made the mistake of acclaiming the Taliban. She's grown mad with it all. Never in a thousand years could she have imagined that the Taliban would be capable of assassinating her son in cold blood and in front of her eyes. Now she picks up pebbles and throws them in front of Taliban cars. They've caught her and whipped her any number of times. But she just starts over again, indefatigably. What does it matter if they beat her? She has nothing left to lose.

In February 1997, I go out for the second time, this time with Soraya. Although they've forbidden women to work, the Taliban have promised to pay them their salaries for several months yet. Daoud accompanies us to the head-quarters of Air Ariana, a few kilometres from home. It's very cold out. We've pulled on long black dresses on top of jogging trousers and sombre sweaters. Our trainers are black, as are our socks. With our nut-coloured burqas well installed on our heads, we should, in principle, escape the Taliban's suspicion.

The main avenue has changed greatly since I last saw it. The television and airline company buildings are still closed and have a sinister quiet about them. They've installed cabins out of corrugated iron a few metres in front of the building doors. These are ordinary container units into which they've cut an entrance reserved for women. It's here that women are received, one by one, to have their ID verified and to collect their wages. Through the door, I notice a kind of peephole. While we queue, the significance of this comes to me. A woman walks through the large door to the inside of the cabin and then stands in front of the peephole through which she slides her hand containing her papers. A Talib outside takes them from her, verifies them and, in the same way, passes them back to her together with her wages.

Burqas are evidently not enough for them. They need even greater protection from women. They need corrugated iron to keep them away. But what exactly are they afraid of? We may be impure, but that's hardly stopped them from slapping a woman barehanded and thrusting her onto a heap of barbed wire!

The women who have come that day to get their wages start to protest. Why humiliate them by refusing to allow them to enter the main building? Why receive them in corrugated container huts?

One of the Taliban who is sitting on the ground at the entrance to the container gets up to fire a round of bullets into the air and frighten us. He certainly succeeds so far as I'm concerned. But Narguesse, a colleague of Soraya's, is beside herself and suddenly pulls off her burqa and starts to scream.

'It's shameful to treat us like this!'

There's general stupefaction around her. She's dared to make the gesture of rebellion and show her pretty airline attendant's face in daylight.

Fired by her passion, the other women round on the Talib and scream their anger. A moment later, more Taliban appear who bundle us roughly into the hut and take away Narguesse, who's struggling like a she-devil.

Once we're locked in, we take off our burqas and shout at the men, 'We won't leave here without her. Bring her back.'

There are about twenty of us, no more. I don't know if Daoud has witnessed the scene. I think not. Persuaded that the wage retrieval formalities would take for ever, he must be walking along the avenue while the row inside the hut rages. We're frightened for Narguesse. We're all asking ourselves what kind of punishment they're inflicting on her. Our only form of pressure is to stay here, our faces uncovered, so that they hesitate to throw us outdoors. It's a rather feeble form of blackmail.

Finally Narguesse reappears. She's very agitated and she's wearing her burqa again, but she says nothing. The Taliban scream at us to leave the premises.

Eight of us are going in the direction of Mikrorayan. On the road back, Narguesse tells us what happened.

The Taliban made her go into the old personnel office on the ground floor.

'Why did you remove your burqa?' they asked. 'Why do you want to be stubborn and insult us?'

'Because you have no right to keep women from working. No right to receive us today in those huts, as if we were stray dogs. We gave our labour to this company, contributed to its working. And we hardly wore burqas, either on the airplanes or in the offices.'

'You're only a woman. You have no right to speak. You have no right to raise your voice. You have no right to take off your burqa. The time when you travelled and walked without a burqa is gone.'

Twice Narguesse made to take her burqa off again and twice they prevented her.

'If you carry on like this, we'll kill you.'

Luckily for her, one of the Taliban who was guarding the hut, came to tell his boss that we refused to leave as long as Narguesse wasn't returned to us. They hesitated only for a moment, then pushed her out.

'Get out. And shut up!'

She'd escaped severe punishment, perhaps even death for having rebelled in this way. Why did they really release her? Through fear of having to dominate a handful of women? It's true, there weren't all that many of them. Maybe, too, they'd received instructions from above, but what instructions exactly?

Narguesse can't calm down. She's scarlet with angry passion. A dear friend of Soraya's, she's always been impetuous and fiercely independent.

'We have to rebel, take action. Today we couldn't do much because there weren't enough of us. But if tomorrow there are thousands of us, we'll manage to topple these Taliban.'

We all agree with her, but how to rebel? Get together, yes, but where? We risk putting our families in danger. We have neither arms, nor freedom of expression, nor newspapers nor television. Whom can we address? How can we get external support if all we are is faceless shadows without a voice?

That was our first demonstration in five months of Taliban rule. I was frightened. I was still agitated when Daoud caught up with our little group on the Mikrorayan road.

That night in our apartment with its blackened windows, we sat in the glimmer of gas light and finally had something to tell Mother about. But Mother, once so combative, only said a little sadly, 'You were brave. Of that I'm certain.'

She rested weary hands on our heads and I had the terrible certainty that she no longer wanted to hear talk of war or rebellion. She only wanted to swallow her medication and go off into leaden sleep. The Taliban can't reach her there.

clean and with a surgical needle sew up
over the chest and torso of this woman.
or has to know how to do more or less
mad world of ours. This woman tells us
ce. She's been whipped by the Taliban's
she dared to go out on her own.
'Why did you go out alone?'
lled in battle during the winter of 1994.
no brother, no son. How am I to live
ne?'
anage today?'
anied me to your place.'
is woman had to go out. But the Taliban
erstand. They simply lash out.
ads to another. They can't stay happy
for long. Soon, they go on to new

ctober 1996, I opened the door on a
crime committed against women.
rom the BBC World Service that the
hmed Shah Massoud had linked up
zbek chief, Abdul Rachid Dostom, his
unch a counter-offensive to the north
aria said nothing about it, of course,
a only glorifies the successes of the
ommits any of their losses to silence.
e the mullah in charge of 'informing'
lic, it would be altogether clear that
quered Afghanistan in its totality at
he truth is that the Resistance led by

3

Three Young Women

The kitchen window and the door of our apartment are now my only points of contact with the outside world. In the morning, I contemplate the mosque and my old school from a distance. During the day, I sometimes open the door to welcome one of my mother's clandestine patients who dare to sneak through the streets in their burqas in order to get her help. Once the consultation is over, I close the door on them again and return to my room to stretch out on the bed and listen to very soft music or watch films I've already seen at least ten times.

Physically, I'm not well. A bizarre and nameless exhaustion nails me to my bed at Soraya's side. We repeatedly evoke all the things we no longer do. Even Daoud's birthday, last October, went by in a muted, unremarkable fashion. That dress I longed for and intended for the wedding we never got to, is folded up in a cardboard box. It'll never be worn under the Taliban.

I find it hard to believe that we are the same people who used to love celebrations, weddings, family reunions, where we were free to laugh and dance. The same people who strolled out into the streets and bought make-up, music, books; who discussed things endlessly with friends on the way home from school. Some of my friends, less modest that I am, openly burst into laughter when boys walked by, whispered appreciation of their looks or clothes. They were only fifteen or sixteen, but some of their parents had already started to think of engagement.

I'm a lot more reserved on the subject of boys. I always thought that I wouldn't marry until I was certain of a boy's character, his past and his family. And certain that I could love him. I'm a believer, I pray, I respect the conventions of our society. If my future husband asked me to wear a headscarf or chador outside the house, I'd accept without a problem. But I would go no further than that in my submission. My parents support me in this.

I know very well that in our culture a woman can't live without a man's protection, whether it is her father's, brother's or husband's. Alone, there's no social life for her. I don't refuse this protection. On the contrary. But I want my independence and the freedom to think. Soraya is unattached. That's essential for her profession. She says she's like me. She'll only marry a man that she, herself, has chosen. Neither my father nor my mother wants to impose anyone on us. In any case, we're in no mood for marriage now. Nor do the terrible times we're living through encourage possible encounters.

We no longer see our extended family. We no longer see anyone except occasionally our neighbours. Since that episode in front of the Air Ariana headquarters, my sister and I no longer go out.

I rage impotently against the Taliban who imprison us. I allow myself to be taken over with the hideous idea that

3

Three Young Women

The kitchen window and the door of our apartment are
now my only points of contact with the outside world. In
the morning, I contemplate the mosque and my old school
from a distance. During the day, I sometimes open the door
to welcome one of my mother's clandestine patients who
dare to sneak through the streets in their burqas in order
to get her help. Once the consultation is over, I close the
door on them again and return to my room to stretch out
on the bed and listen to very soft music or watch films I've
already seen at least ten times.

Physically, I'm not well. A bizarre and nameless exhaustion nails me to my bed at Soraya's side. We repeatedly
evoke all the things we no longer do. Even Daoud's birthday,
last October, went by in a muted, unremarkable fashion.
That dress I longed for and intended for the wedding we
never got to, is folded up in a cardboard box. It'll never be
worn under the Taliban.

I find it hard to believe that we are the same people who
used to love celebrations, weddings, family reunions, where
we were free to laugh and dance. The same people who
strolled out into the streets and bought make-up, music,
books; who discussed things endlessly with friends on the

way home from school. Some of my friends, less modest that I am, openly burst into laughter when boys walked by, whispered appreciation of their looks or clothes. They were only fifteen or sixteen, but some of their parents had already started to think of engagement.

I'm a lot more reserved on the subject of boys. I always thought that I wouldn't marry until I was certain of a boy's character, his past and his family. And certain that I could love him. I'm a believer, I pray, I respect the conventions of our society. If my future husband asked me to wear a headscarf or chador outside the house, I'd accept without a problem. But I would go no further than that in my submission. My parents support me in this.

I know very well that in our culture a woman can't live without a man's protection, whether it is her father's, brother's or husband's. Alone, there's no social life for her. I don't refuse this protection. On the contrary. But I want my independence and the freedom to think. Soraya is unattached. That's essential for her profession. She says she's like me. She'll only marry a man that she, herself, has chosen. Neither my father nor my mother wants to impose anyone on us. In any case, we're in no mood for marriage now. Nor do the terrible times we're living through encourage possible encounters.

We no longer see our extended family. We no longer see anyone except occasionally our neighbours. Since that episode in front of the Air Ariana headquarters, my sister and I no longer go out.

I rage impotently against the Taliban who imprison us. I allow myself to be taken over with the hideous idea that if they stay in power for much longer, my entire life will be done for. Unless we flee our country to join the growing mass of exiles and refugees, something my parents refuse to contemplate. I'm with them on that.

Our only consolation is my parents' relative affluence. It offers us a layer of protection that many other women, forced to go out into the streets, envy us – even if it's only the privilege of eating when we're hungry. But as the years pass my sister and I will grow old without work, love or children. My sister is sad, at once resigned and pessimistic. As for me, the internal revulsion that rages through me has become a sickly inertia.

There's a knock on the apartment door. I recognize its brusque insistence. It signals a clandestine patient and says as clearly as words, 'Open up quickly. Shelter me. I don't want to be seen.'

To be seen? Who recognizes a woman beneath a burqa? But fear among women is now so prevalent that it's become second nature. Fear of meeting a neighbour, of answering a question. We're suspicious of everything. I open the door to a brown burqa. The woman pulls it off as soon the door is shut. Her face is swollen, her lips puffed and bleeding. She doesn't need to speak. I lead her to the living room where my mother examines her. Out of respect, I leave them alone together. But I hear the woman crying through the shut door, and a few moments later my mother calls me. 'Bring some boiling water and bandages. Quick.'

I fill a pot, prepare bandages and wait for the trembling of the water impatiently. Yet another woman humiliated and beaten. God only knows why.

I watch Mother clean and with a surgical needle sew up the wounds that cover the chest and torso of this woman. A clandestine doctor has to know how to do more or less everything in this mad world of ours. This woman tells us of the latest injustice. She's been whipped by the Taliban's cable-lashes because she dared to go out on her own.

Mother asks her, 'Why did you go out alone?'

'My father was killed in battle during the winter of 1994. I have no husband, no brother, no son. How am I to live if I can't go out alone?'

'How did you manage today?'

'A cousin accompanied me to your place.'

To feed herself, this woman had to go out. But the Taliban don't bother to understand. They simply lash out.

But one thing leads to another. They can't stay happy with just beatings for long. Soon, they go on to new methods.

At the end of October 1996, I opened the door on a new horror – a new crime committed against women.

We had learned from the BBC World Service that the Mujahidin under Ahmed Shah Massoud had linked up with those of the Uzbek chief, Abdul Rachid Dostom, his ancient enemy, to launch a counter-offensive to the north of Kabul. Radio Sharia said nothing about it, of course, because Radio Sharia only glorifies the successes of the Taliban heroes and commits any of their losses to silence. If one were to believe the mullah in charge of 'informing' the Kabul radio public, it would be altogether clear that the Taliban had conquered Afghanistan in its totality at least twenty times. The truth is that the Resistance led by

Massoud still holds about 25 per cent of the terrain the Taliban want to annex. The struggle continues and is located in the region of Kohestan.

A few days after this news came through, at about nine in the evening, I open the door to four burqa-wrapped women. One of them makes herself known to me instantly. She's Nafissa, an old school friend of Soraya's. The three others, who are young girls, are her cousins from the provinces. But they refuse to uncover their faces. Nafissa briefly explains that they came from the region of Kohestan, from the plain of Shomali to be exact.

As they've arrived alone, my father is worried. 'Is there no one with you?' he asks.

'A taxi driver agreed to bring us here.'

Mother ushers the three girls into her living room and closes the door, while my father silently goes downstairs with Nafissa to thank the taxi driver.

I hear the three girls crying and my mother's voice urging them to be calm and not attract the attention of neighbours. Then she comes out of the room, writes a quick note and calls Daoud. 'Take this to my friend, Dr Sima, in Mikrorayan two, and hurry, Daoud – we've only got an hour until curfew.'

After ten, we're no longer allowed to move around the city and all lights have to be out in the houses. As an extra precaution tonight, despite the fact that our windows are blacked-out so that no one can see into our apartment, we drape heavy dark material in front of the windows to allow Mother to examine the girls safely.

Then Mother asks us to stretch a long roll of plastic on

the floor so that she can operate. As there are no new surgical needles in the house, because Mother can no longer get supplies from the hospital as she used to do, we boil water in order to sterilize old needles. After that, Mother places them in a flask of alcohol. I still don't know what's wrong with these three young girls who are curled up on the floor and sobbing silently into their burqas. One of them sways lightly to and fro while holding on to her stomach. The picture of the suffering despair of these three girls will stay with me forever.

While waiting for Daoud to return, Mother joins us in the kitchen and tells us what's happened to them.

'They're around your age, Latifa, fifteen, sixteen. The Taliban took them hostage during the offensive on the plane of Shomali. A gang of about fifteen men. They raped them . . . all fifteen of them. It's horrible, outrageous . . . But that's not all. They . . .'

Mother pauses. We understand that's it's difficult for her to recount such things to her own daughters. Soraya has tears in her eyes. I stare fixedly at my mother, so shocked that I have to stifle my cries.

'What? . . . What did they do?'

'They mutilated their genitals. Ripped them . . .'

She won't say any more and goes back quickly to look after the three tortured girls. She needs to disinfect them now, anaesthetize the area and sew them back together again with what tools she has. I don't even dare ask her if the girls can withstand the pain. I don't even dare imagine . . . I utterly reject this vision of a gang of fifteen brutes savaging three girls of my age, three virgins. My sisters.

Daoud comes back just before curfew accompanied by Dr Sima. When he takes in the scene, the poor man reacts so violently that Mother has to ask him to control himself and keep his head.

'You have to help me finish up. Calm yourself. Did you bring what I asked?'

'Yes, everything I have.'

From ten at night till four in the morning, they take care of the girls and sew them up. From our room, we can hear the patients' feeble moans and the whisperings of Mother and Dr Sima. It's impossible to think of anything else. It's impossible to sleep.

In the countryside, young girls don't have the same sort of life as we do. My mother experienced it during the Soviet occupation. The administration sent her to work in Kandahar for six months. She was in charge of public health – preventative measures, as well as care. She told me how difficult it was to talk about birth control, gynaecological problems and even about female anatomy. A woman of around forty came to see her one day and complained of hot flushes and various pains. She was convinced that she was pregnant; in fact she was menopausal.

The future for these girls in their region was a marriage arranged by their family. Rape had killed that future. No neighbour from their village, not even a cousin elsewhere in the clan, would come and ask for their hand in marriage. No one. And even if they somehow managed to keep the whole thing secret, their lives would be marred by the brutal weight of an intimate shame.

To violate an Afghan woman is to oblige her to marry

her rapist, according to the cruel tradition that is still practised today. Or to condemn her to exile or death. I'm not of a violent disposition but that night, I recognized that if something like this happened to me, I could easily kill my rapist before putting an end to myself.

Their painful work finished, my mother and Dr Sima are sitting in the kitchen over a cup of tea while the three girls in the living room finally drift off to sleep. My mother is persuading Dr Sima to open up a clandestine consulting room.

'There are too many sick women in the neighbourhood for me to handle everyone myself. They even come from far away, as you've seen. I don't have sufficient material or medicine. You, your children are grown and live abroad. You could ask them to send the medicine we haven't got. You could organize all that far better than me. On top of it all, I'm exhausted. I haven't the strength or the energy.'

In Kabul the postal service is reduced to its simplest function. The smallest package risks being seized. So everything comes by messenger through Peshawar in Pakistan. That's the transit point for any money or goods that Afghans abroad send home to their families or friends. Even messages and letters often take that route. Of course, you have to make sure of the messengers and have a safe channel, which is true in Dr Sima's case. In urgent situations, every time Mother has needed medicine since the arrival of the Taliban, it's thanks to Dr Sima that she's got it.

Dr Sima doesn't hesitate to accept Mother's proposition that he set up a clandestine surgery. After the horror that he's just witnessed, the urgency of it is evident. And then there are Mother's usual patients, who no longer have anywhere to go because of our very own catch-22 – that only men are doctors and doctors are only authorized to treat men.

That night saw the beginning of the most important clandestine medical surgery in Kabul. The three girls left in the morning with Nafissa and the taxi driver. To what fate? We never saw them again.

Every day our world grows a little more degraded. It rots around us without our being able to battle against the process. Father tells us there are more and more beggars in the streets. Most of them are women forbidden to work or widows. My school friend Anita's mother does people's laundry to earn her keep. She used to be a teacher at my senior school. Other women bake bread or make traditional pastry that their sons sell in the street. Others do embroidery or beadwork.

Daoud recently saw boys selling loose cigarettes as well as single aspirin tablets. He also tells us that other youths have taken to drug dealing in order to help their families survive. Drugs, on the frontier with Pakistan, are the most lucrative form of trade and the Taliban let it happen. All this while, Radio Sharia spouts out yet more decrees. Mullah Omar, their chief and their master thinker, has now decreed that the embroidered lattice work which allows women to peer out of their burqas, has stitches which are too big. From now on, the stitches have to be smaller and tighter. The mullahs haven't yet indicated the exact size we need to respect. It'll probably be less than half a millimetre.

With this added aberration, I lose all confidence in myself. So does my sister. Over and over again we repeat, 'But what can we do? What can we do? Should we just die?'

I've been really ill for quite some time. This morning I'm running a temperature and I'm terribly dizzy. If I try to get up, I fall back on my bed. Mother thinks my blood pressure is zooming down, but she doesn't understand why. The worst thing is that she's far more ill than I am.

Depression has enfolded her more and more deeply. We take care of her the best we can, but we have so few means at our disposal. And the only medication to hand is sleeping pills. My father, who loves her so much, makes sure he's by her side every possible moment. To lose Mother would be too awful. She's always run everything in the house. She used to be so organized, so efficient, a woman of remarkable spirit. On top of everything else that's going on in Kabul, there's the added grief of seeing her like this. The constant worry weighs heavily on each of us.

The only time when Mother seems all right is when she can take care of someone or give them advice. Sadly, sometimes she prefers not to see her suffering patients. She has nothing to give them that will help.

Recently, a woman suffering from excessive bleeding came to see her. To cure her, Mother would have needed a medicine that cost approximately 1,200,000 afghanis (£179.00), even if one could find the medication. Before the Taliban, she would have easily purchased this kind of medicine from the hospital. Now, she can't even go there. Excluded from her profession, she'd be thrown out and also punished. This prohibition on her nurse's practice torments her all the time. She even has dreams about it. When she had to send the woman home with no help, she said to us, 'That woman will suffer complications. It's inevitable. She'll probably die of some gynaecological infection, even though it would be so simple to prevent it. One injection. That's all that's needed . . .'

A medical practitioner's conscience isn't put to rest very easily. And we understand Mother's pained bewilderment. That a simple medical problem can lead to a woman's death because of a Taliban decree is more than discouraging.

As the summer of 1998 begins, my poor father has two sick women in the house: his lethargic medical wife who is incapable of taking care of her ailing daughter. In any case, the mysterious illness that makes me run a temperature is not in her line of expertise.

My father calls a doctor friend and begs him to come and help. He's a man, so he isn't allowed to treat women, and he's frightened. He'll come on one condition: that Father swears to keep it secret. That's all he wants as payment.

The doctor can do nothing for Mother's depression. But he suspects there might be some diabetes at play, although she's never been diabetic before. He does blood tests for both of us and takes the phials with him.

'I'm going to give these to the laboratory under my daughter's name,' he says to my father. 'But I can already tell you that both of them need to be taken to a hospital in Pakistan and treated immediately. Latifa is also depressed, but on top of that, she's got pleurisy. There's water on her lungs. You mustn't wait too long.'

In fact I've been ill for about three months, with interim periods of feeling better. The temperature has only recently moved in to stay.

So, it's decided. We're going to go to Peshawar, but the organization of the trip takes time. A car has to be found and a driver, amongst other things.

At last everything is ready. Father packs Mother's bag, while Soraya prepares ours. Daoud is staying home to take care of the house. Apparently the Taliban are eager to move into apartments like ours that are modern and in the privileged neighbourhood of Mikrorayan. We're going to stay with Chakila's parents-in-law during our period of treatment.

In normal times, going to Peshawar doesn't pose any particular problems, apart from navigating a particularly dangerous road and the rules against Afghanis leaving the country. Despite this, many Afghanis regularly go there, once or twice a month, in order to purchase supplies. The customs officials shut their eyes. The system of getting to Peshawar involves pretending that you're going to Jalalabad, negotiating strict controls at several points on the road to the frontier – a line which Pakistan has unilaterally modified in its favour. My elder brother often said that Pakistan had long dreamed of annexing our country.

It's our first trip since the Taliban took power. Our first trip in almost two years. Summer has arrived and the weather is very hot. Our burqas are stifling, but we three women have to wear them.

At dawn the estate car and its driver are waiting for us outside our apartment building. If I weren't so ill, this trip would be a distraction. But I'm feeling apprehensive about it, not only because of the dangers of the road, but because Mother is more and more exhausted.

The driver warns my father again, 'Above all, don't forget to say at the control points that we're going to Jalalabad.'

The road that cuts across our suburban neighbourhood of Kabul tells the history of our country since my birth. It's littered with the carcasses of Soviet tanks. The walls bear the marks of Mujahidin gunfire from the siege of Kabul under Commander Massoud in 1992. Mines and grenades still dot fields and roads.

At the first checkpoint as we leave the city, we have to get out of the car to have our papers inspected. We also have to submit to a physical search. For men, the search is carried out according to the rules by the guards themselves, who do it seriously. For the women, the Taliban enlist little boys as young as eight, since they are the only males who are allowed to approach us. As women aren't allowed to work, there can hardly be any policewomen.

The child doesn't even address us. He simply signals for us to lift our burqas, examines our faces quickly to see that we haven't transgressed by wearing make-up, and vaguely runs his hands over our long skirts. The search stops there. The boy looks serious, slightly contemptuous, but he is probably proud of his work, despite his youth. The rifle he wears on his shoulder is almost bigger than he is.

What kind of man will he grow into?

Then, it's time for the search of the car boot and our

cases. My father shows his case. The guard opens and inspects it carefully.

'Where are you going?'

'To Jalalabad.'

Our fear is almost tangible. These Taliban can have such unexpected reactions, particularly towards women, that anything is possible. Mentally, I go through the contents of my case. I've only brought dark and black things with me. No colour. So have Mother and Soraya. In principle, women's cases aren't searched; the Taliban are too pure to touch female clothing.

As soon as my father says, 'That bag is my wife's and those two, my daughters',' the guard steps back.

The line of cars is long both in front of and behind us. We have to wait another twenty minutes before we can go. When we do, the jolt affects my back, and from time to time, Mother asks Father to instruct the driver to go more slowly. The sun rises high in the sky and it turns very hot. We reach the region of Sarowbi after about two hours of exhausting driving. Here there's another checkpoint and we submit to the same routine. Then we're back on the winding road again in the direction of Jalalabad.

As we near the city, there's a third checkpoint. Each time we're stopped, our anxiety keeps us silent, attentive to the guard's smallest gesture. They can stop us or send us to prison without our even knowing why. It's enough for one of these men to get angry at a single traveller for however small an infraction of one of their laws, and all the rest of us would suffer the consequences.

A little ahead of us, we see a bus being searched. The

Taliban are making the women come out and then the chauffeur is told to do an about-turn.

The suspicious look the guards cast on our documents, their way of examining them, almost make me appreciate my burqa, even though it all but prevents me from breathing in a temperature of forty degrees in full sun. Once this checkpoint is finally crossed, we still have to confront the mountainous road to Samarkhail, which has more twists and turns than a serpent in a figure of eight. When we reach the town, there's a fourth checkpoint to get through. Our worry, our fear of being stopped has hardly lessened.

Near the Turkham Pass at the frontier, we see little boys coming back from Pakistan carrying jerry cans full of petrol or oil and sacks of sugar with which they will do business. Men are sitting on the ground with piles of Afghani currency for Pakistani travellers and Pakistani rupees for the rest of us.

It has taken us over seven hours to get here and Mother is utterly spent. It's at this moment that the driver says to us, 'Hurry up. They're going to close. And I can't go any further.'

We have to take our bags out of the car, find a boy with a cart to transport them and attempt to make the rest of our way on foot up to the point where we reach the heavy black and sinister metal gates which block our passage.

Father and Soraya are holding Mother up to help her walk. She proceeds slowly, too slowly, stopping at each moment to regain her breath. And we're not sure at exactly what time the customs officials will close the border crossing. My father is also watching the young man who's pushing the trolley with our cases too quickly.

At last we're in front of the black gates, covered with asphalt and barbed wire. There is no other way through unless one scales a steep mountain. In front of these doors, there are armed Taliban. On the other side, there are armed Pakistanis. Travellers go through in groups. We hear it said that the border will be closed between twelve and one in the afternoon. We have just about enough time, give or take a minute on either side.

A Talib rifles our luggage, examines my father's passport, the only document that testifies to the existence of his wife and daughters. Prohibition or no prohibition on leaving the country – that's all a mockery. Here, thousands of people cross the border. The important thing is that there's a man to deal with and that the women are appropriately submissive in their burqas, their heads bent and mute.

At that moment, a Pakistani policeman comes out of his sentry box and makes ready to close the border. Behind us, a woman cries out, 'Let us through, brother. Don't close the gates.'

The Talib looks back. He comes toward the Pakistani and addresses him so violently that the man withdraws without a word and instead of going into his wooden sentry box, he goes to hide behind it in fear of the Talib who might fire off some bullets in his direction. Even this official is scared.

But he isn't scared of my father. As soon as we're on the other side of the crossing, he comes up to him with a colleague. He has a self-important air. There's a gun strapped across his back and he's waving a stick in front of him, his fists clenched at either end of it.

'Your authorization?'

My father hands him his passport. There is no authorization and the Pakistani knows it full well. He wants something other than a document. He wants money.

'Where are you going?'

'To Peshawar. My wife and daughter need treatment.'

My father resists because he hates this corrupt system of giving money to an official for no reason except greed. In fact this territory belongs to us. The Pakistanis simply stole it. They're not at home here and they know this so well that they attempted to get Najibullah to sign an official document recognizing this new frontier before killing him. I know what my father is thinking at this very minute in front of this Pakistani thief. He's thinking, 'You're in my country and you dare to demand payment from me, an Afghan. This is no mere racket. This is an outrage against Afghanistan.'

But the frontier is here, even if my father can't stand it. What he can't stand is that it became the new frontier so easily and without any country in the world making a fuss about the change. Finally he takes out a fifty rupee bill.

The customs official shakes his head. 'That's not enough, sir. It's fifty rupees per person.'

This time, my father loses it. His voice rises. 'What is this? What do you want? Do you want me to make a scene here? Is that it?'

The man is angry, but he finally gives in. 'All right. Just give me fifty. Get on with you.'

Fifty Pakistani rupees is hardly an enormous sum, less than a pound. But it's a question of principle with my father. Under the Taliban, Kabul operates as a cash economy, and my father can only get hold of money thanks to the good graces of his associate in Peshawar to whom he has given a small amount of capital for his business.

He's furious. Once the bribe has been paid, he mutters through his teeth, 'That's the last time I come to Pakistan!'

We now have to find a taxi to take us to Peshawar. The driver we find looks congenial. He starts to talk to us immediately. In Kabul, no taxi driver talks to his passengers. There's too much mistrust around.

'You're from Kabul?'

'Yes.'

I'm Afghan too. But I've been living in Pakistan for the last eighteen years . . .'

We're in a car going along a free road in a free country and, despite the heat, the steep, serpentine curves, the road is in far better condition than on the other side of the border. There are dangers, of course. At the bottom of the ravines, you can see the remains of trucks or buses. But the slopes of the mountains are green. There are trees and wild flowers. The driver stops for a moment near a fresh water reservoir that sparkles and plunges downwards over the rocks. Here we can finally rinse our faces. I'm suffocating. My sister too. Our feet are swollen from heat and too much sitting. I lift up my burqa to sprinkle cold clear water on myself, though it's apparently better not to drink it.

This brief mountain stop is a true delight. I've hardly eaten or drunk anything for the length of the journey. The water on my feverish cheeks is a gift from God. To walk around freely without the Taliban is like a miraculous breath of oxygen. It could almost clear my lungs.

But despite this taste of liberty, we keep our burqas on until Peshawar. We still need to be careful.

The driver is talking with my father. 'I understand you. The situation in Afghanistan is ghastly. The Taliban are bad people. They oppress with too many laws.'

Father asks him to drive slowly for Mother's sake and we take off. Soraya and I stay silent, our eyes wide on the scenery. The driver has put on some music. It escapes from the car's open windows. By two o'clock we're in Peshawar, which we approach through the Karkhana zone.

In front of us, further than the eye can see, there are endless rows of shops full of merchandise on several floors. The driver talks to us about this immense bazaar which deals in all kinds of goods: it's a site for trafficking a vast assortment of products which come from everywhere, a zone unto itself, lawless, free of taxes and customs duties.

'Here, you'll find your drug and arms merchants. That's all this lot of stalls handle. Further on, by the checkpoint, you'll find household goods, cameras, televisions, radios, tape recorders, air conditioners. Anything you want.'

On another of our borders, the tribes import merchandise into Afghanistan without paying any customs duties, because we have none, or very little. These goods are then re-exported into Pakistan, also with no duties to be paid . . . That goes for arms too.

It's clear that our country, devastated by years of civil war, serves as a comfortable haven for Pakistani trafficking.

That's why Pakistan had no hesitation in recognizing the government of the Taliban – to whom they supply soldiers with the agreement of the United States. We'll all be dead if the Resistance doesn't take control of our capital again. Our country will be wiped out, swallowed up, under the cover of that very special Sharia instituted by the Taliban.

When we get to Chakila's parents-in-law's house, my sister hugs us and weeps bucket of tears. She hasn't seen us for ages. Nor has she experienced the arrival of the Taliban, but of course all this time she's been continuously worrying about us. She feared she might have to join her husband in the United States without having seen us again. In Peshawar, people know more or less what is going on in Kabul, but Chakila wants to know how we spend every minute of our days.

'How do you cope with the burqa?'

'We don't go out.'

'It must be very hard on you. You're so young. But what do you do at home?'

'I read. I've tried to take up my English studies again with the books you sent me.'

'Are you doing it alone or with Soraya?'

'Alone. With a dictionary.'

'You're thin. Mother too. Much too thin and very weak.'

Chakila asks for news of our uncles, aunts and cousins as she takes us towards the house's bathrooms. There are three of them. Water pours out of the taps. We'll be able to take a real shower – a luxury we hardly remember in Kabul. Chakila busies herself. She brings us towels, soap. Her sister-in-law helps out.

Then Mother goes to stretch out on the sofa and Chakila gently massages her feet until she falls asleep.

My sister is soon going off to the United States. She's impatient to join her husband, but has little knowledge of the country in which she's going to live. She only knows that her husband has taken up a business in Virginia. America is an unknown planet for us – the way of life, the people, the names of cities, we learned nothing about all that either under the Soviets or later. Chakila is sad at the thought that she might never see Afghanistan again. But she trusts her husband. She loves him.

There, she'll no longer be a journalist; she'll work in her husband's shop. They'll keep our traditions going. She'll wear her headscarf to say her prayers under a sky that isn't ours, that's all.

Meanwhile, Chakila gives us news of old school friends who have come to live here. They're at university, lucky to be pursuing their studies.

But we can't come and live in Pakistan. Chakila will soon leave and for my father, it would be inconceivable to ask for asylum from the in-laws of his eldest daughter. His pride couldn't take it.

The next day, at the hospital, I go to one clinic, Mother to another. I'm given an X-ray. The doctor examines it and asks me, 'Why didn't you come for treatment sooner?'

He must know, I imagine, that in Kabul a woman can't be treated. But he asks the question as if it were somehow our fault.

I'm hospitalized for a week. They make a puncture in my lungs to draw out the water – two bottles filled with a strange liquid. They give me vitamin B and other medicines whose names I don't know.

Father comes to the room I share with another sick woman and says sadly, 'They confirmed your mother was severely diabetic. For her depression, the doctor could only prescribe sedatives. He's keeping her for two days, then I have to take her to a neurologist. There isn't one in this hospital.'

Mother thus leaves the hospital before I do. Her visit to the specialist isn't comforting. My father has to explain to him what she herself can't formulate. He knows very well that she won't speak about her inner ordeal – she doesn't speak of it even to him. Nor does Father manage to relate in detail the succession of shocks and strains she has undergone, because there are Pakistani guards in front of the doctor's door, and an Afghan never feels able to talk freely in such conditions. He fears he'll be overheard and it will result in political difficulties.

Mother was a happy woman before the arrival of the Soviets. Her career and her married life were both successful. My parents loved each other with a love that has never grown weak. But after the Soviet invasion, there were too many misfortunes to contend with: my eldest brother denounced and imprisoned for three years; Daoud, who needed to be hidden so that he wouldn't be forcibly enlisted; the daily horrors of the civil war, first in her work as a nurse, then as a gynaecological specialist. And now, the suffering of all those women she had tried to help during the long months of the Taliban regime . . .

How to explain to a Pakistani doctor what happened to

Daoud at university after the battle between the various Mujahidin factions that lasted from 1993 to 1996? I remember every movement of my mother's face as she listened to Daoud's story then. I was twelve. It was so frightening, I've never been able to forget.

Daoud's faculty was closed and occupied by the allies of Hekmatyar, against whom Ahmed Shah Massoud was then battling. They used the building as a barracks. Hekmatyar lost and when the forces of Commander Massoud took control of the zone, the radio launched an appeal to students asking them to come and clean the premises so that they could be opened up again. Daoud went one morning with all the other students who wanted to take up their courses once more. A lot of them turned up voluntarily.

When he came home, Mother instantly saw that he wasn't well. He was very pale and wouldn't talk. He holed himself up in his room without eating. Mother was still in the kitchen and she insisted that he join us.

'Come and eat, Daoud.'

'No, I'm not hungry . . .'

'What's wrong with you?'

Daoud didn't answer. That was worrying, so I followed Mother into my brother's room. He was sitting on his bed, his hands covering his face. Mother sat next to him, waiting until he could speak.

'I saw something that shocked me,' he said at last. 'Something really horrible.'

'What did you see?'

'I saw a woman completely undressed . . . She was . . . she was nailed to one of those swinging doors at the faculty.

They had cut her in two . . . in two parts. On each panel of the doors, there was half of her. Half of her nailed-up body . . . And the door opened and shut. It was appalling. Horrible.'

Mother started to cry. Daoud went on.

'There were feet. Hands cut up. Bleeding remains here, there, and everywhere. It was a massacre. I don't know how many they killed, but it was terrifying . . . The radio only said the students should clean the building, put things back in place. But we couldn't clean, not that. We just couldn't. The security guards ended up doing it. I don't want to go back this afternoon. I can't. They sent us there so we could see what the others had done. They wanted us to know, but . . .'

I went to my room to weep alone. Daoud never mentioned any of this again. But Mother still thinks about it. She can't stop. I'm certain of that. And there are a great many other nightmares I don't know about that she locks up in herself. She doesn't say anything. Just contains it there, all pushed down and deeply buried. The newspapers talked about the massacre at the university later, but they didn't give any details.

The specialist advised my father to watch Mother carefully to make sure she was taking her tranquillizers and the medication for her diabetes. She was also told she had to walk for at least two hours every day.

At the end of a week, I feel better. I can go out. The doctor has also told me to walk for at least two hours a day, and to exercise in the fresh air as much as possible.

As my father said to him, 'Apart from the medicine, we can't really do much . . .'

At night at Chakila's in-laws, we three sisters talk things over. The temptation not to go home again, to stay here and flee our country is great. Seen from the outside, our government looks even more appalling.

But it's impossible. Chakila is now set to leave for the United States. She's just had a phone call from her husband. Her papers are about to arrive. Her in-laws can't keep us here. As for Soraya and me, it's unthinkable that we'd let our parents return to Afghanistan without us. There we've got a roof, an apartment where we can pay the rent. In Pakistan we'd be free, Mother would be looked after, I'd go to university. But there's a negative side, as Chakila points out.

'People look down on us here. Even though all business in Peshawar is run by Afghanis. Even though we've built houses, made the economy turn over, the Pakistanis don't like us.'

And it's true.

Meanwhile, every second day, I make use of the fresh air and take my walk. We've bought cloth to make clothes with, real black summer shoes to replace our trainers, and Father has offered me a prayer shawl. We chat amongst ourselves in the garden at sun set. A real family. A real life.

But after a month, we have to go home. Mother, Soraya, and I find it very difficult. I leave behind the image of my old friends trotting off to the faculty, laughing, walking without obstacles through the streets of Peshawar or

Islamabad. Most of them have a brother, an uncle or a close family relative living abroad, who can help them financially. Not that their life is luxurious. A friend told me over the phone that there were seven of them sharing a single room in Islamabad. Still, she's fortunate to be able to study. I hope she's aware of her luck and works as hard as she used to. During our conversation, I had the feeling that she had lost some of her drive to become a doctor. She seems more superficial, less concerned than she used to be. Maybe that's one of the things that freedom does.

We make the journey home in a bus as Mother and I are feeling better. The searches, the roadblocks, the Taliban with their evil looks, the constant humiliation . . . I feel even more deprived than before our departure.

Mother now refuses to take the pills for her diabetes. My father and Soraya think of all kinds of ploys to make her swallow them. She prefers her tranquillizers and sleeping tablets. We watch her as we would a child. Mother, once so strong and active, refuses to confront reality. She wipes it away with sleep that grows deeper and deeper. We no longer know what to do as her depression wins over all four of us.

We feel even more dejected when Daoud tells us that the football he so loved in the Kabul stadium has given way to the performance of a new Taliban atrocity. Now justice takes place in public. They hang the accused from the goal posts, cut off the hands of thieves, execute supposedly adulterous women with a bullet in the back of the neck. This is a monstrous spectacle, intercut with obligatory prayers. Spectators are forced into the stadium with whip lashes.

I don't want to hear any more about the horror in my city. I won't leave the apartment any more. I'll content myself by looking out the kitchen window and sleeping as much as possible, like my mother, in order to forget the nightmare lived out under the blazing sun of Kabul.

4

Massacres And Miracles

It's BBC time, 8.30 p.m. Father switches on the radio and turns the sound down as low as possible. We all gather closely around the set so that we can hear. One day the neighbour across the hall overheard us and remarked on it to Soraya, 'Your radio is too loud . . . I heard that the Taliban . . .'

Soraya cut him off by apologising instantly for disturbing him. 'My sister and I must have had the music up too loud. We're so sorry.'

The neighbour didn't mention it again, but we're suspicious on principle.

The important town of Mazar-e-Sharif, in the north of Afghanistan, has for a year been the site of fierce battles between the Mujahidin of the Northern Alliance and the Taliban. If the Taliban, who are laying siege to the city and who have suffered heavy losses there since they took power in Kabul in 1996, succeed in their present action, this will mark the downfall of the last of the northern citadels not yet in their hands . . .

The world service broadcast confirms the rumours racing round Kabul about which we can never be certain. Even when a reporter manages to interview one or other camp, it's difficult to get a clear picture of the situation. Whatever the Taliban affirm, is instantly denied by the heads of the Resistance. Sometimes, too, the broadcasts are inaudible. In the morning, for example, between 5.30 and 7.30, at the time when Iranian radio is transmitting, our sound is completely scrambled. They say in Kabul that the Taliban do it on purpose, because Iran gives lots of air space to the advances of the Resistance. If anyone in Kabul is caught listening, he's liable to three months imprisonment.

For some time, the news has been demoralising. In February 1998, an earthquake hit the north of the country in the region of Taloqan and right up to Tajikistan. Only the BBC gave us the toll of dead – 4,000.

Radio Sharia gives us all the news on the supreme justice of the Taliban: two criminals have been personally butchered in the Kabul Stadium by the father of their victims. The Taliban themselves estimated the public who watched this prime spectacle at 35,000. Luckily they don't use television to bring the event into our homes. It's at moments like this that I don't miss the TV.

The news that most worries my mother concerns the departure from Kabul of a humanitarian organization run largely by women. They were chased out by the Taliban. This non-governmental organization represented Afghani women's last resort in the search for medical aid. The women who worked there are accused of not bowing before the

Islamic law which forbids work, studies and medical care to women. Mother is aghast.

'That's the end for women. The very end. There's nothing left. It's genocide. And the UN allows itself to be black-mailed by these Taliban.'

Soraya no longer speaks. She moves sadly around the house offering no comments. Father's efforts to tell her that her professional expertise won't disappear from lack of practice, that one day she'll work again, no longer have any effect. She doesn't believe him. Our country seems to have been altogether forgotten. No one is interested in us. Journalists are so rare. It makes us think that the world approves of the Taliban.

In August 1998, Radio Sharia – which we can listen to in the morning without fearing our neighbours' big ears – triumphantly announces the capture of Mazar-e-Sharif near the border of Tajikistan and Uzbekistan. The Taliban have occupied the sacred city – site of the blue mosque that shelters the tomb of Ali, the Prophet's son-in-law.

'Thanks be to God who is great, we unify our country. All the cities of the north have now rejoined the government.'

Radio Iran then takes over to accuse the United States of supporting the Taliban in order to degrade the image of Islam. The Taliban, we learn, have massacred hundreds of civilians in the sacred city and kidnapped some Iranian diplomats. My father says simply, 'They're preaching jihad. But a Muslim doesn't kill another Muslim. Nowhere in the Koran is it written that we should take life. This is the final proof that they're inventing their own Sharia, all the while wanting us to believe that whatever they decide is written in the Koran. Their laws aren't written in the sacred book. They come out of the heads of a few mullahs who would do better to keep them for themselves.'

I go and stretch out next to Soraya who's sleeping, her pretty face covered by the sheet despite the heat. I think about the way things used to be, about Mazar-e-Sharif and the magnificent trip there that my brother Wahid organized when I was about twelve.

It was my first journey within Afghanistan and the only one until now. I was so happy to go off with my admired big brother and with Mother and Chakila. Father stayed home with Soraya, since both of them had to work. We went to spend the Afghani New Year holiday, Nowroz, which begins on the first day of spring, in the city which houses Ali's tomb. We stayed for a month.

I remember a spot on the road where uniformed men searched the bags of travellers. One of them asked our driver, 'Where are they going, these people?'

'They're going to Mazar-e-Sharif, to the big mosque.'

The man stretched a cash box in front of him.

The driver put a few bills into it without saying anything and we went off.

Wahid had rented his car for the three of us for the whole journey. The driver was a kind man. Before we set off, he said to us, 'Just tell me if you want to stop anywhere to see something or go to the toilet and I'll stop.'

At the beginning of the drive, there was nothing around us except desert. Looking out the window, I saw two youths, a little taller than me, perhaps fourteen. They were carrying Kalashnikovs. As our driver kept on going, one of the boys threw himself in front of the car and held up his hand to stop us.

'Why didn't you stop before?'

'No one asked us to stop.'

'Park your car over there and give us some money.'

The driver again gave money. Then he said to us, 'If you're thirsty, I'd advise a stop after the Salang peak and the tunnel. The water's good there. It comes from the mountain snow.'

The water was marvellous, fresh and clear and the scenery was magnificent. There were houses hanging from the edge of the mountain and we could see people walking up and down from the furthest peak along a narrow path that snaked between the trees. We ate delicious kebabs. Our driver insisted that they were better in the north than anywhere else.

After lunch, we got into the car again and just before arriving at Pul-e-Khomri, I saw the house of my dreams, the one I drew over and over again when I was little. It was a grey stone house with a smoking chimney, a sheep-fold and a well, set in the very midst of the greenest hills. I would have loved to live in that valley, surrounded by trees. Everything was calm, silent. It was so beautiful.

Wahid had told me that the next village we came across was called Dacht-e-Kilaguyi, which means 'banana'.

'You often talk to us of this place.'

'Are there a lot of bananas here, then?' I asked.

'No, not exactly. There are a lot of watermelons.'

We laughed. A few minutes later, the driver said to Wahid, 'Give me your watch and your mother's. All your watches.'

To Mother, who asked him why, he replied, 'Madam, if you have any jewels, you have to give them to me, because very soon we'll come to a place where thieves may stop the car and take everything from us.'

After having hidden the watches and jewellery in the boot, he started to drive briskly. 'If anyone throws a stone at us, don't worry. I'm not going to stop.'

As we drove along, I saw a stopped car, surrounded by thieves. Because the thieves were preoccupied, we got through untouched.

At the entrance to the sacred city, a large banner announced, 'Welcome to Mazar-e-Sharif'. The people were all Uzbeks in traditional clothes – a thick brown shirt they call a gopitcha and a round, very long turban. I had already seen some Uzbeks in Kabul, but that day it seemed to me that many resembled each other and had a particular 'Mongol' look. The women weren't all wearing burqas. Some had headscarves on, others nothing at all.

We went to a hotel to rest. There were so many visitors in town that we almost couldn't find a room for four. But after a little discussion with one landlady, Wahid got what he wanted.

Wahid was quite bossy. Sometimes at home he argued with Chakila and they then wouldn't talk to each other for two or three days, without our parents realizing. It was their own business and my sister didn't want to trouble Mother with all that. With me, Wahid was different. He would take me to the amusement park and to the bumper cars, with my little cousins. He teased us non-stop. He showed us postcards of Indian movie stars by the light of his pocket torch and made us pay five afghani each, as if we were at the cinema. Or else he'd invent bank accounts and would have us deposit our money with him in exchange for a phoney cheque. Daoud would laugh and call him a crook, because we all knew he was earning a little extra for himself so he could go to the movies on his way home from school. By the time we went to Mazar-e-Sharif he was twenty-five.

Wahid's face has changed with the years. He doesn't laugh anymore. He's become grave, altogether serious. Mother says he suffered too much. For me, Wahid is a walking history of our wars. Maybe that's because he's the soldier in the family.

He did his studies at the Ansari senior school, then went to military college. He graduated top of his officer class and was attached to the presidential guard regiment. To finish up his training, the Soviets sent him to the Front in a troop that operated at Maidan Shahr. He stayed there about three weeks. At that time, the most active fronts were those of Kandahar, Maidan Shahr and Wardak. Wahid told us when he got back that the Soviet soldiers massacred civilians before their very eyes. That they shot children and old people with no provocation. In certain villages, when women threw stones at them, they responded with Kalashnikov fire. He was utterly depressed by the experience. My mother later told me that she cried more than once in listening to his stories. Every time he had to go back to the Front, she shook her head sadly. 'He goes off as one goes off to commit suicide.'

In two years, Wahid took part in over 104 operational missions. But during that period, he was also confined to barracks several times for rebellious behaviour. His punishment consisted of spending several days in a tiny and very low tent, on wet open ground. You could only stretch out flat or stay crouched over, but you couldn't stand. Wahid was then under the orders of Colonel Hazrat, his teacher, who praised Soviet aid to Afghanistan repeatedly and demanded blind obedience from his men to any orders from Soviet officers. Wahid rebelled against Soviet orders and was often less than polite to his teaching officers. He would say things like, 'Afghanistan has enough men and officers to do without Soviet additions.'

At one point we had no news from him for several weeks. Mother sent Daoud to the barracks where he learned that his eldest brother had been condemned to five months in a cell for having thrown a teapot at his colonel. After that, they transferred him to another division stationed in Paghman at the limit of the security zone to the west of Kabul.

One day a mullah from the council of ancients, a very old man, came to see my father at home.

'Your son has done remarkable work for us and I've come to thank you.'

When Father saw his son come home on leave wearing traditional dress and sporting an Afghan beret, he understood what had been going on, but he asked nonetheless.

'What did you do to make me worthy of the thanks of the Mullah of Paghman?'

Wahid had been charged with guarding the Paghman part of the security belt around Kabul. After the victory over the Soviets, the Afghan Resistance controlled almost all the country regions and the Communist government in Kabul did all it could to defend the big cities, the roads and airports. Hundreds of soldiers held position on the hills around the capital. Normally, the army didn't permit villagers to cross this security zone to go and buy produce in Kabul. But Wahid let them get through. Unfortunately this was transmitted to the Khad, the Soviet government's secret service. General Farouq Yaqoubi, number two in the secret service, called in Wahid. My brother explained to him why he behaved as he did.

'The army taught me to serve the people. And so I allowed the people's representative through. If you don't think that's appropriate behaviour, why don't you give my post to the informer who spied on me.'

He wasn't dismissed that day. I imagine that his answer was embarrassing for a Soviet, who in principle was meant to defend the people. But now Wahid knew he was being spied on by the Khad. In fact, he had already been 'solicited' by the Resistance because his post was such a key one in the security zone round Kabul.

After two years of active service on the Front, he was transferred for two months to a military base situated in Fronze in Kyrgyzstan. Every weekend he'd come home, take off his uniform, put on his traditional robes, don his pakol and go and pray in the mosque.

One day, a certain Sangar, the brother-in-law of President Najibullah, who lived in a neighbouring building in Mikrorayan, stopped my brother in the street. I was nine then. I was with my parents on the terrace, and we saw them in the distance talking for some two hours. My father was fretting because this man, so close to the president, also ran a branch of the Khad.

As soon as Wahid stepped into the house we bombarded him with questions.

'So, what did he say?'

'What did he want?'

'Nothing. Not much. All trivialities of no importance. Stop worrying.'

Wanting to reassure us, he gave us no meaningful response. But a little after this, he vanished, and we had no news of him for over three weeks. We imagined that he had been sent elsewhere without having been given the opportunity to tell us. But one summer night, a soldier from his division came discreetly to our house. He talked to Chakila and went off again. I insisted on knowing what he had said, but Chakila wouldn't answer. 'We have to wait for Father.'

Finally at dinner, Chakila announced the news. 'Wahid is in prison.'

My father went into a rage. He was furious that the army hadn't alerted him. He telephoned Hashim, a family acquaintance who worked in the personnel service of the Khad, and they agreed to meet the next morning to go and find Wahid.

The commander of the Paghman garrison, General Issa

Khan, who was in charge of Wahid's division, told them he was being detained in Block Two of the prison of Pol-e-Tcharkhi, which is reserved for political prisoners. We were overwhelmed. This was the most tragic event to have befallen our family. Wahid was a political prisoner of the Soviets.

My father went to the prison, but the first time, he couldn't get permission to see Wahid. The soldier on guard could only take the clean clothes my father had brought and, at Father's behest, he agreed to bring him Wahid's laundry.

On the inside of his trousers, Wahid had hidden a piece of paper on which he had written, 'Father. I'm alive. You have to get a letter of permission signed by the Minister of Defence in order to see me. Wahid.'

It took almost a month for Hashim to obtain an authorisation signed by the Minister for the entire family to pay Wahid a visit.

There were terrible stories about the tortures carried out in the Pol-e-Tcharkhi prison. One of my uncles, Mir Akbar, my mother's brother, had been detained there in the seventies. He had told of the torture he had undergone, his back gashed and scarred, his nails pulled out . . .

The Pol-e-Tcharkhi prison building is very different from the old prison in Kabul that is made of earth-coloured brick. This prison is a veritable fortress in Soviet style, built with the arrival of the Communists. We could see it as soon as we arrived on the plain some fifteen kilometres outside Kabul. It was enormous, so big that a car could drive on top of its thick external walls.

Hundreds of people were queuing to see their loved ones. I was stupefied. I had no idea that there could be so many people in prison. I asked myself why?

Two hundred metres from the entrance, two checkpoints held the police charged with controlling visitors. One was for women, the other for men. After an hour's wait, our name was called. We went into the checkpoint building where a woman stamped each of our arms in turn. Father was stamped in the same way at the men's checkpoint.

The woman searched us, then gave us the authorization to walk towards the huge iron gate. It stretched so high that I had to bend over backwards in order to be able to read the inscriptions at its crown. 'Central Prison of the Democratic Republic of Afghanistan' and 'The Prison, Second School for Reapprenticeship'.

How were we to understand the words 'school' and 'apprenticeship'? I couldn't really make out what one could learn in prison.

Each time we went to see Wahid, not only did we have to queue for our stamp before getting through the crowd, but the same operation was repeated several times once we were inside. We went through six iron doors. At each stage, the guards checked the men's stamps and signed their skin in confirmation. By the time we got to the end of the long hall, my father had two stamp marks and six signatures on his arm.

After that we were led to an open courtyard at the centre of the building. The ground was wet to prevent the dust from rising. My brother's name was shouted out and finally he came towards us. He stretched a shawl on the ground and we all sat down. I devoured him with my eyes. He wore a beard and black clothes. We all cried. Wahid kissed my mother's and father's hands and begged us not to cry. We only had half an hour and he had things to tell us, but we were watched by an armed guard who listened to our conversation so that Wahid could only tell us the essentials.

He had already been interrogated. He needed a lawyer in order to go to trial. And he wanted our uncle, Mir Akbar, to defend him. He recommended that my sisters always wear a chador, as well as long traditional dresses like those we had on that day. He had always insisted on this, but this time Chakila didn't have the heart to start arguing with him. Finally, before leaving, Wahid embraced us and murmured, 'There'll be men watching the house. You mustn't be frightened. There are three of them and they're there to protect you.'

He gave us his dirty laundry and we left him without having understood why he was in prison and why men would be keeping a watch on us.

My uncle was the prosecutor in a military tribunal. Because of his job, he knew army regulations extremely well. And because he'd spent some time there, he also knew the rules of prison life. When he came to our house, the first thing he asked us was whether we had taken home my brother's laundry. He immediately started to search through the package to take out strips of paper from the folds in the trousers. Wahid's notes asked him to come and visit him personally in the prison and as soon as possible. They stated that he wanted only our uncle as an advocate.

I found this means of communication staggering.

From then on, every Wednesday for three months, we went to see my brother in prison and sat in that courtyard on the damp, rich earth. Wahid said the guards kept it wet to obliterate the traces of blood. There was also blood on the walls.

Much later, after the arrival of the Mujahidin of Massoud in Kabul, we were shown a horrifying documentary on the television. Digging in this fertile soil, men found the corpses of prisoners assassinated without trial. Without knowing it, we had been walking and sitting in a paupers' graveyard.

Each visit, Wahid told us stories of prison life. There was a chief guard, prepared to give him certain facilities for payment. He was called Khiali Gul . . . This man came to find my father in his store one day. He took money away with him and that very night, Wahid telephoned us at home. He could talk for a long time. He was in Commander Gul's room. He asked for a small television set, which astonished us, because we didn't think it was authorized, as well as an antenna with a cable three metres long so that it could be linked from his cell to the roof of the prison. When it arrived, there were no problems installing it.

Once, when we were with him in the courtyard, he pointed to a prisoner. 'His name's Ghazi. He's the prison hitman. For 5,000 afghanis (75 pence), he'll kill any condemned man. I was told that Commander Abdul Wahid, one of the great leaders of the Resistance, was captured during an offensive in the valley of Panshir. Ghazi gunned him down right here.'

One autumn day, when it was raining cats and dogs, the

95

prison was suddenly invaded by a squad of armed soldiers. A prisoner had managed to escape dressed as a woman in a long burqa.

On our way out, the guards examined every woman before letting her pass through the gates. Tanks were stationed in front. On our visit after this escape, we women got two stamps on our arms instead of one. Wahid told us that the prisoner had escaped by fabricating a false stamp out of potato peel and a black felt pen that his wife had brought him. Before being arrested, he was a specialist in false documents.

On another day a commotion broke out between political prisoners of opposing Resistance factions who were incarcerated on the same floor. A new detainee had been assassinated. The weapons used were sharpened bones. The prisoners had dug into a pile of food scraps that had been dumped in a corner of the courtyard, and there had found the basic material for their killing tools.

Another prisoner died when he had boiling water thrown in his face by a fellow inmate. Another still, in Block Four, the toughest of the wings and one reserved for major criminals, set fire to his clothes with petrol before rushing off into the prison courtyard. He hoped that his act would bring the intervention of the International Red Cross and fully intended to jump into the reservoir he knew was just behind a gate. But that day, the gate was closed and he was burned alive before the other inmates, who stared at him from behind their bars.

One young prisoner, sentenced at eighteen for theft, was offered up as fodder to rapists by a hardened criminal from

Block Four. The man worked in the kitchens. The victim took his revenge by cutting his throat with a meat cleaver.

Chakila listened to my brother's stories with the curiosity of a journalist. Soraya often cried and I . . . well, I asked myself what kind of world this was, so very distant from God.

One day, Chakila brought home a clairvoyant, the mother of one of her friends. After having felt my brother's clothes and done some complicated calculations based on his date of birth, she announced, 'Wahid is a pious and wise man, a good Muslim who says his prayers. In four months, he'll be free.'

Her conviction was so great that even Mother was impressed. She wanted to pay her, but the woman refused. 'Until my prediction is fulfilled, I don't ask for anything.'

I didn't believe in her at all. Father only said that it was good for Mother's morale. It was January 1992. Wahid had been condemned to twenty years in prison, a sentence my uncle only managed to reduce to eighteen. He had now been in prison for three years and I kept asking myself what could set him free apart from the grace of God. My sisters and I prayed fervently every night.

Then, on 18 April 1992, General Baqui, the chief of the Khad and General Yaqoubi, his deputy, both of them close collaborators of Najibullah, were assassinated.

I was in school when Chakila arrived to ask permission to take me home. She'd heard that something was going on and knew that it would be safer to be together. In Mikrorayan, where a lot of Afghan Communist party members lived, news circulated quickly. On top of that, the area is situated between Radio Kabul and the international airport and is close to the Presidential Palace. Then, too, Chakila was a journalist.

That evening, when we turned the television on, there were only patriotic songs to be heard. At about 7.30, a presenter appeared and stated, 'Dear compatriots. Dr Najibullah, the former Afghani president, who wanted to leave Afghanistan illegally, etc etc. In order to avoid a power vacuum which would enable the Pakistanis to seize our country, we are now in permanent contact with the Mujahidin . . .'

At that moment, we had no clear idea whom the government would contact to fill the power vacuum. And then one morning, while Chakila and I were out walking, the greengrocer said to us, 'Commander Massoud is coming to Kabul. Everyone in town is talking about it.'

The population had been dreading the arrival of Hekmatyar's men, because they were the ones who were raining rockets on Kabul. The next day, on the evening news, the Minister for Foreign Affairs appeared on the screen. 'I've just been by helicopter to Panshir where we've been negotiating the transfer of power. Gulbuddin Hekmatyar and Ahmed Shah Massoud have agreed to a ceasefire as they enter Kabul.'

The next day on my way to school, I immediately noticed a number of changes. Our teachers were wearing trousers instead of skirts and tights, and they had long coats or heavy chadors on. The girls were all discussing last night's developments.

'If Hekmatyar's extremists take power, the war will go on.'

'The condition of women will change. We won't be able to work.'

'The schools will be closed.'

I didn't dare say anything because my brother was in prison and I feared that my words might do him harm. I feared that Wahid's ideas put him with the extremists.

Two days later, uniformed men appeared in our neighbourhood. Some of them had even taken up position in a corner of our school. Because they wore military uniforms, the girls in my class had no inkling that they might be Mujahidin.

The same day, some of our neighbours, particularly those who worked in the Ministry of the Interior, started bringing things home with them – television sets, rifles, tape recorders, radio-cassette players. We all felt raids and looting were about to begin. Men started to let their beards grow.

Television continued to function with male and female presenters. There was still music. But on the evening of 28 April, the female presenter, even though she still had make-up on, already wore a head shawl. That was new for us. Several days later, Sebghatullah Modjaddedi was designated president of the new Islamic State of Afghanistan.

On 5 May, the doors of the prisons were opened: political prisoners and criminals were amnestied simultaneously. That evening, Wahid appeared at our door. He was bearded and in traditional dress. Even though he had just come out of prison, he was more aware of developments than we were. He was happy, and so were we to see him. But the next day he went to the market and came home with three enormous chadors that had nothing in common with the headscarves we had worn until then.

It was then that Chakila said to him, 'All right then, we'll wear your chador, since it seems to have become the height of fashion.'

It was the following year that the two of us and Mother went with Wahid on the pilgrimage to Mazar-e-Sharif to take part in the New Year celebrations which coincide with the festival of the red tulips – Gul-e-sorkh in Afghani.

When we arrived in Mazar-e-Sharif, the spectacle was superb. Around the city, there were fields full of red tulips perched on tall, slim stems – a veritable living collection for Soraya! I had never seen anything like this blood red ocean glistening in the sun.

We visited the great mosque with the blue cupola and gazed at the ancient basin whose stones are engraved with verses from the Koran. The outer sanctuary was of a pale blue marble lined with deep red and as smooth as a mirror. All around it white doves were perched. On this New Year's day, pots of red tulips stood everywhere. I was overwhelmed by the beauty.

Some pilgrims, blind or disabled, had been praying here throughout the year waiting to take part in the New Year festival in the hope that a miracle would occur on that day. Inside the mosque, there was a giant Koran placed on a lectern. One could leaf through it to find a passage one wanted to recite, but some people were reciting verses off by heart, without consulting it. We made a donation to the mosque and then went off to pray at the tomb of Ali.

Chakila asked a woman what we were meant to do next.

She answered, 'This is Ali's temple. You can pray and ask something of God. Your wish will come true, since he's a maker of miracles.'

I prayed for Mother's health and asked God to protect our whole family. Then we saw a strange thing: hundreds of padlocks hanging from a metal bar. What on earth could they be for? I wondered and again we asked someone.

'You have to choose a padlock and pull on it. If it opens, your wish will come true. My sister-in-law did it a few days ago and she asked that her husband, about whom she was very worried, come back to Mazar-e-Sharif. That very night, he came home.'

Chakila refused to pull on a padlock. I would have done it willingly, but she tugged my hand away just as I was about to touch one.

'I don't know what any of this is about, Latifa. I've never seen anything like it. Rather than do something stupid, it's better not to touch these padlocks at all.'

Wahid was waiting for us outside. He had gone to pray in the part of the mosque reserved for men.

We bought seed to feed the blue mosque doves. I noticed that there were lots of tourists, even Westerners who were marvelling at the beauty of the place. There are mosques just as splendid and just as large in Kabul, but this one is unique and particularly venerated because of the tomb of Ali with its miraculous properties.

By an extraordinary chance, Chakila and I witnessed a miracle. Some men had hoisted a flag in front of the vast crowd. Sick and handicapped people were praying just in front of us. Suddenly a man lifted his hands to the skies, then rubbed his eyes and started screaming like a lunatic that he had recovered his vision! Immediately the people around him rushed to tear at his clothes, which were now sacred. The man thanked God, all the time rubbing his face. He gazed at the sky in ecstasy as more and more people crowded round him. He allowed them to tear at him. I saw hands raised respectfully towards him, but others were more insistent in their supplications. I began to fear that he would have no more cloth to give them. But he seemed altogether unaware of the ferment around him. He was dazzled by the light and he kept on trying to hide his eyes behind his hands and then lifting them off again, all the time crying, 'Thank you, thank you, my God.' His family protected him as best they could.

I was utterly stupefied. I tugged at Chakila's sleeve and repeated, 'Look, Look, it's a miracle!'

'I'm looking. Let go, you're hurting me.'

Mother was too far away from us at the moment to share our emotion, but she saw what happened and she too was persuaded that it was a miracle. Later on, a man who worked at the mosque told us that this pilgrim had been praying there every day for a year.

Wahid too was impressed, but much calmer than we were. 'God is truly great,' he said gravely.

When we returned to Kabul, I immediately recounted this marvellous story to Father.

'I once saw a miracle, too,' he said. 'A man had a paralysed leg and he started to walk before my very eyes. There are often miracles at Mazar-e-Sharif.'

This August night in 1998, I find it hard to imagine miracles and to sleep. They're talking about massacres in the holy city. There are hundreds of dead. It isn't the season for tulips. They'll have long lost their bloom. The Taliban won't have seen the red flowers spreading their blood towards the sky. They'll have spread blood, instead, the blood of the men and women of Mazar-e-Sharif. 'God is great,' Wahid said, 'and thanks to the mediation of Ali, the blind recover their sight.'

If I could address a prayer to Ali in front of his marble tomb at the blue mosque, I would implore him to perform a miracle for the poor Afghani people, abandoned by everyone. I would implore him to teach the Taliban – who dare to invent inhuman rules, contrary to the holy book, these Taliban who are utterly ignorant of the teachings of the Koran – to respect the holy book as we have always humbly done.

5

The Little Girls of Taimani

One morning I prepare tea in the kitchen for my friend
Farida who has come down from the sixth floor to chat
with me. She thinks I should be reacting more to the situation, that I'm letting myself go.

I no longer have any fever, my lungs are better, and for
a while now, Farida has been harassing me to emerge from
my depressive inertia. She always wants to shake me up
and raise my morale. She goes out from time to time,
whereas all I do is drag myself around the family apartment moving between my mother's illness and Soraya's
sadness.

We open the kitchen window in order to get a little air,
and through the bars, I look at the mosque as I often do.
The building work is finished now, perhaps thanks to Bin
Laden's gifts, just as I said in my exam paper.

Mosques have become the strongholds of the Taliban.
They teach their version of the Koran inside them. I see
the mullah at the centre of the courtyard. He's surrounded
by little boys who tirelessly recite at his command. This
mullah holds a stick, undoubtedly so that he can hit any
child who makes a mistake or hesitates.

Farida watches it all with me. 'What if he's making them

recite complete nonsense? Look at the poor little boy. He's just rapped him over the knuckles.'

It's at that precise moment, as we sit looking out of this small window, that my student's brain suddenly wakes up. First, the children in the Koranic school are, of course, boys. On top of that, all these children can learn from a mullah are the texts of the Koran. Religious education is important, of course. It's always been part of the curriculum, but when I was a student I was taught a great deal more – history, geography, Persian literature, maths, science. Who's going to teach these boys all that now?

Schools for boys still exist, but they're no longer obligatory. Some parents must still think that a minimum of education is better than none at all. But how good can this impoverished education be? The Taliban's propaganda has taken hold of everyone so quickly.

For the first three years of school, boys now have to wear a little hat and the traditional pyjama. At eight or nine, they have to don a white turban, still much too big for them. Many of the boys in our neighbourhood are no longer educated, because their parents simply assume that their courses are selected and vetted by the Taliban. In addition, if the mother is a widow, then forget education altogether. Her sons have to help her by selling whatever they can in the streets, or begging. For these women, isolated by the system, a son is a means of survival.

I was lucky compared to these children. My schooling only stopped with the arrival of the Taliban. I went to primary school at five under the Soviet occupation. From my ninth to my twelfth year, the civil war between the

Mujahidin and the Communist regime had little impact on my studies. Under the Islamic State instituted by the Resistance, I did my finals and undertook the university entrance exam in journalism.

Now I'm eighteen and for two years I've lived this cloistered life in which I do nothing at all. Yet I could have been useful by passing on even what little knowledge I've already garnered. Farida is thinking along the same lines as I am this morning. Maybe she's been thinking this way for a long time.

'Listen, Latifa,' she says. 'For you and me, it's finished now. We won't be abe to study any more. But we could do something for those children. At least we could give them some clear ideas to set against that mullah over there.'

'A secret school? Like Mrs Fawzia's?'

One of our former teachers was recently caught in the act by the Taliban – right in the middle of teaching a class. First they beat the children, then they hit her. They threw her down the stairs of her building so violently that she broke a leg. Then they dragged her by the hair and jailed her. And after that, they forced her to sign a declaration promising that she wouldn't start again, that she respected the law of the Taliban. They threatened to stone her entire family in public if she didn't acknowledge the error of her ways.

I admire that woman enormously. She taught me a great deal when I was a pupil. In creating her secret school Mrs Fawzia knew what she was doing and the risks she was running. The children would never come to her at the same time for their schooling; nor did they leave at the same time. They left their books at her house. Nothing illegal, according to the decrees of the Taliban, was visible on the outside.

Mrs Fawzia must have been denounced by a neighbour or a beggar. These last are on the watch for any information they can give the Taliban; it's their way of currying favour. Yet Mrs Fawzia was so prudent. At the start of each class, she would say to the children, 'Keep a text from the Koran next to you. If anyone comes into the room, you'll have to say that's what we're studying, and that's all we study!'

The sight of those little boys in the mosque, reciting while they sway forwards and backwards, terrorized or hypnotized by the mullah, that's the trigger I somehow needed to react to my situation. Sometimes that's the way of things. It's like destiny. Farida proposes that I replace Mrs Fawzia and take up where she left off. It would be a small revenge for her to know that someone has taken up the torch. Farida and I discuss the way we'll proceed, how we'll set up our school along the principles established by our former teacher.

'We'll have to talk to her to establish the curriculum she followed, find out where she left off.'

'We'll only take pupils in our building sector. We'll choose people we know well and on whose discretion we can depend.'

'We'll have to enlist some help from friends too. Maryam, for example, I'm sure there's nothing she'd like more.'

'Each one of us will give courses from home. Dispersal will act as another form of security.'

At last I have a goal. We prepare a note for Mrs Fawzia

that we send to her in secret. It's more prudent not to go to her house or to ask her to come here. The poor woman is handicapped since her imprisonment and can only move with difficulty.

She answers us very quickly. She accepts our proposition with joy. Not only will she give us a curriculum to follow, but she can come from time to time to help us out. After all that's happened to her, it's clear she's unbelievably courageous.

I feel stronger after we've taken this first step and I tell my father and Daoud about our project. Farida tells her father and her brother, Saber. It would be impossible to proceed without the approval of our families, who will have to accept illegal pupils in their houses.

Everyone agrees on the project, but Daoud also warns us, 'It's fine for Mrs Fawzia to give you materials, but if she comes here it'll only rouse suspicion. You're putting her life at risk. If she gets caught a second time by the Taliban, it's curtains for her. You haven't the right to do that to her.'

Both our families agree that Mrs Fawzia should not come and help us out at our homes. We do begin, however, as soon as she sends us her course plans.

Farida and I each take ten pupils. Our friend Maryam will have five or so, depending on the day. Our pupils are between seven and fourteen, girls and boys both. We're taking risks of course, but they're limited. The children won't have far to go. They're all from the immediate neighbourhood. Some of them won't even have to leave the apartment building, which has thirty-six flats. This proximity is essential for their security.

One of my cousins who lives in the Taimani borough of Kabul told my father a story that struck us forcibly, more than justifying our caution.

For the little girls of Taimani, there was a clandestine school about half an hour away. The children took risks in getting there. One day the bodies of several of them were found in a rubbish dump. They were only seven or eight years old. They had been kidnapped, raped and strangled with their own clothes. I think a lot about the little girls of Taimani as we organize our project. It's in their memory that I want to help the children of our neighbourhood.

Despite her weakness, Mother has a sudden burst of energy and encourages us. I try and protect her from the noise of the children as they come and go at different times of the day. But I think she appreciates our efforts even more because she can't practice her own profession.

Soraya has promised to correct the children's homework in the evenings. Daoud busies himself getting the material we need – pencils and notebooks. Each family gives us a sum of money so that he can stock up at the stationer's. The only problem is books. We can find them, but they're expensive: 12,000 afghani for a simple school text. Given the inflation we're suffering, this is an enormous sum. So the parents of the pupils each buy a manual for their children, according to their means. Maryam covers mathematics. Farida and I do reading, writing and history. Another friend dedicates herself exclusively to English classes for the teenagers.

At the end of the morning classes, I watch the street from the window. If I see anyone I don't know, or who looks suspicious, the children wait before leaving. Often they even eat with us. Then I let the biggest boys leave first. After another careful scouring of the street, the girls leave together; the young brother of one waits to leave with them. Curiously, I'm not frightened. I carry out these tasks serenely, as do my friends. The network is water-tight; we know the children's parents, the children are highly motivated and know exactly what they're up to in this improvised school. They know it's a secret to keep and understand its importance in the intellectual desert of the Taliban regime. They carry nothing with them, neither notebook, book, nor even a pencil, when they leave the apartment. I keep everything in my room. And they come to class in the same way, at irregular moments, and as empty-handed as if they were going for a walk from one building to the next.

I start working between nine and ten, depending on the children's arrival, and classes stop at noon. My room has become the classroom. Religion, history and geography, Persian literature and, twice a week, writing and dictation. I have five girls. Ramika is fourteen and the only one to wear a burqa. Kerechma and Tabasom are twins of seven. Malika is six and Zakia, five. The three boys are younger. Chaib is seven, Chekeb and Fawad, five.

Imitating my own childhood teachers, I always start the day in the same way. 'Have you done your homework? Anyone who hasn't, please step to one side and we'll take care of it afterwards.'

I continue with, 'Today we're going to talk about the importance of water on the earth and in human life. What is water useful for?'

As I speak I see myself as a pupil again, listening to my teacher. Mother registered me at the school in Mikrorayan 1, on the banks of the Kabul River. I did all my primary classes there. Every morning at eight, Father took me to school. Chakila came to fetch me at about 11.30.

In my class there was a girl called Wahida. She came from Kandahar, the big city that overlooks the Rajistan desert. As she was older than the rest of us, the teacher had designated her head of class, an honour that should have come to me as my grades were the highest. I thought she was too bossy, but, of course, I envied her. When Wahida announced that she was going home, she expected me to be sad. On the contrary. I remember saying to her, 'It's good for you to go back there.' I became head of class and took great pride in it.

When I think about those days again, I see that I wasn't a particularly nice girl.

Throughout primary school we all wore traditional clothes, but at the beginning of secondary school, we switched to a uniform made up of a brown dress on top of white dungarees. The Soviets had just built a modern building in Mikrorayan, which they called the Friendship High School. Six months later, they built two more on the same model. School became compulsory, and various measures were used to encourage families to educate their children. They made a welfare payment of 1,500 afghanis per month per pupil and in the senior schools clothes were freely distributed: there were blue dresses for girls and grey shirts for everyone. This system functioned for only six months. We called it Emdad, or 'disco benefits' because the disco fashion of the eighties was, for us, synonymous with the luxury that came from the Soviets.

When the army withdrew in 1989, the Soviets left behind a number of 'advisers' in every field. We nicknamed them 'those who missed the boat'. We had a lot of Soviet teachers in our senior school during the occupation, but in 1989 there were only two left who had 'missed the boat'. One of them taught my class. My friend Farhad, who was always confident, regularly provoked this teacher by launching paper missiles at his head.

'Why do you stay behind when everyone else has gone?' he asked him.

As Farhad's father was an important member of the new party in power, no one dared reprimand him. I thought he was badly brought up. After a while, these last two teachers left as well, though I don't think Farhad's paper balls had anything to do with it. His hatred of the Soviets was understandable.

In our neighbourhood, a lot of children lost their fathers during those years. They had either died, gone to prison, or had disappeared. There was Fereshta, Yama, Aymal and Babrak, my playmates, and above all, Anita, who made me so sad . . . Anita and I were in the same class for nine years in a row. I liked her a lot. She was a slim girl with pale skin and chestnut hair, always charming and sweet-tempered. When I learned she had been orphaned, we grew even closer. Her father had been arrested by the Soviets. No news had come from him since. Her mother couldn't find out why he had been arrested or where he was detained. He was probably in Pol-e-Tcharkhi, like my brother Wahid. But Anita's father, unlike thousands of others, never came back. Her only memory of him was a picture in which she was a toddler in his arms. Her mother cried when she showed it to me. Oddly, Anita didn't react like her mother in her sorrow; she lived on the surface, like a dreamer, adored taking part in school theatre and sometimes sang for the class. It was her means of surviving and living in hope. She often said to me, 'He'll come back one day.'

Compared to her, I was lucky. My parents were alive and I knew their entire history, thanks to an aunt who never tired of telling me about it all. My parents had married for love when Mother was a student in medicine, taking free courses the German doctors gave at the Goethe Institute at Kabul while following her practical nursing course at the Mastourat Hospital. That's where my father met and fell in love with her. For some four years, although he sent her poems and did everything to be charming to this beauty she was indifferent to him. She was only aware of his kindness. It was one of her colleagues who opened her eyes for her.

When Mother fell in love with him at last, her family opposed the marriage. So did Father's grandmother, because she feared having such an educated woman in the family, one who'd worked in a hospital and might not respect her sufficiently. Finally my father said to my mother, 'If they carry on opposing our marriage, too bad. I'll kidnap you.'

In the end, they won their case and had a wonderful period of engagement. Father took his fiancée to the movies, for walks, and to restaurants. A friend of my mother's who worked in the police force remarked to her one day, 'Alia, you chose a real man. The proof is that he's not afraid to take you out to a restaurant!' At that time, my aunt explained, it was thought that men took only loose women to restaurants.

My parents were married in 1964, and we were all proud to have been born of a marriage like theirs. Such is our family history, which reflects Afghanistan's history, and which neither successive wars, nor the battles between ethnic groups, have managed to rupture. Father is a Pashtun, Mother a Tajik. Their union is a symbol in itself.

One morning, in the mid-winter of 1999, the parent of a pupil asks me, through his son, to do a class on the war against the British. Parents often propose subjects they want me to deal with. Given the age of their boy, I keep my account simple.

'The British tried to invade our country, but Afghanis don't like foreign invaders. And so, despite the fact that the British had sophisticated arms and the Afghanis only had sticks, they managed to resist with courage. The British knew nothing about our way of life. I'll give you an example. They had noticed that Afghanis often chewed a dry ball of something that resembled earth, but which they took out of their pockets. This intrigued them. They wondered what use it could be.'

'What was it, Latifa?'

'In the countryside, they pick blackberries, dry them, pummel them into powder and turn them into a sweet edible paste which can keep for a long time. This is called talkhan and it was used to give the soldiers strength during battles.

'After their defeat by the Afghanis, the British didn't take talkhan with them. They took gold, jewels, precious antiques. But they didn't know how to transport them through the mountains, so they disguised them and hid them here and there along the route.'

Another day, there was a different question.

'My father told me that King Habibullah Khan did nothing good for our country, unlike President Daoud. He wants to know what you think about that . . .'

'We'll talk about it tomorrow.'

I was taken aback and didn't want to answer without checking my facts. I also wanted to consult with my family about what one was to think of this historic episode. The next day, having done my revision, I could answer the pupil.

'Your father is right,' I told him. 'That king didn't serve his country well. In his palace he had three hundred women for his pleasure alone. His son Amanullah Khan proclaimed independence and chased the British from our soil, but President Daoud had other ambitions; he wanted to turn Afghanistan into a developed country, modern and independent. For example, he wanted us to be able to manufacture cars and other things of that order. That's why he wanted, not to be king, but president of a republic. Unfortunately he had little time to build on his plans, because the Soviets arrived.'

While I was at school as a pupil, history courses began with the Anglo–Afghani war. After that came the 'modern' epoch in which my parents themselves had lived, under the reign of Mohammed Zahir Shah and then, after he was deposed in a military coup in 1973, the government of his cousin Daoud.

I remember my history teacher, who had explained the nineteenth-century Anglo–Afghani war to us, had suffered a curious slip of the tongue and switched things round when making a historical comparison. 'The Soviets,' he said, 'left Afghanistan in 1878, just as the British did in 1989. Whoops. Sorry. Well, in any case they left in the same manner – vanquished and in retreat.'

The winter of 1988–9 is one I remember particularly well. The Soviets were on the point of leaving the country. It was colder than ever before in Kabul. There were almost no supplies left in the city. The Resistance had been engaging in a politics of encirclement and siege of the capital and we had shortages of everything. With my sister, I'd go and queue separately, in front of two bakeries in order to buy six rolls. Same thing for petrol, because the electricity pylons had been destroyed by the Mujahidin, and everyone had to use mulch for cooking and coal for heat. Everywhere the queues grew longer and longer. We waited half days to get the smallest thing. Some people started queuing at 3.00 p.m. and finally got to the front of the line by 7.00 p.m.; others installed themselves in front of the shops well before dawn, at 3.00 a.m., say, in the hope of getting something by 9 a.m. This misery lasted for four months and people simply died by queuing.

When there was no more bread, the rich ate cakes or pastries. And this was the revolution we had been told about! I ate cake to the point where I felt quite sick.

The Soviet planes could only land at night with their supplies for the capital. The newspapers spoke of Kabul under siege. Between the rocket fire, the interminable queues, the price of rice, sugar and flour, inhabitants' nerves were more than on edge. They got angry on the smallest pretext and fought amongst themselves. Many only thought of leaving Kabul.

Some people gave their daughters in marriage to boys who lived in the west, thereby preparing the eventual exile of the entire family. Others tried to sell all their possessions in order to finance a clandestine trip abroad. Kabul had lost all that superficial joy it had known under the Soviet regime.

Then, in the spring of 1989, the radio announced that goods now filled the shops and all our supply difficulties were at an end. Curiously enough, we Kabulis then had little idea of what was going on in the countryside. Television gave us lots of entertainment programmes at the time, as if to distract and hypnotize us. There were concerts, the election of Miss Afghanistan or Miss Kabul, Indian films . . . Theatre functioned, radio stations poured out music. From time to time, we'd notice that there were more people in the streets, but we knew nothing about all those families who had been forced to flee their homes and villages, because of the ongoing war between the forces of Resistance and the government armies. The population of Kabul was swelling before our blind eyes. We didn't want to see reality. Of course, the Mujahidin existed. Of course there was a Resistance, but we all somehow hoped that the situation would magically rectify itself, that a union between the pro-Soviet regime and the resisters would be arranged, that peace would return.

Then there was Jalalabad. During the summer of 1991, two years after the retreat of the Soviet troops, the Resistance threw itself into a major battle to take the city. It had massive support from the Pakistani army. The Afghan army and the Communist government mobilized all their forces. It was on this occasion that Dr Najibullah gave his famous speech on Ariana Square. The government had to defend Jalalabad against the attacks of the Resistance, of course, but above all it had to fight against Pakistan's interference in our country. Women were enlisted to ensure the security of the capital. It was the first time that I had seen women in military uniform. They were everywhere – at intersections and on big avenues. They worked in the Kabul silo that functioned twenty-four hours a day in order to ensure bread production. They drove the electric trams. They worked in the administration and in banks and sang on television. The girls in the Communist Youth groups went round schools to collect gifts for our soldiers. The mobilisation even won over young amateur singers who gave free benefit concerts for the greater glory of the military. That's when we got to see Madonna clones and Michael Jackson copycats singing for the Afghan army. What I wasn't aware of, was that there were young girls in my neighbourhood who were greatly saddened at the thought of their fiancés going off to the Front.

On the eve of the arrival of the Mujahidin at the end of April 1992, we were invited to a wedding at the Hotel Kabul, situated in the city centre opposite the central bank and nor far from the Presidential Palace and the Treasury. Celebrations started around four o'clock. Both girls and boys were in western dress and dancing. We ate while we waited for the religious ceremony to begin. Suddenly a soldier burst into the room and demanded to see the father of the bride. The officer announced that Mujahidin units had penetrated the capital and that the marriage had quickly to be concluded. The majority of women were wearing décolleté dresses and their husbands hurried to cover their shoulders with their own jackets before rushing home.

Five minutes later, everything was over. The elder brother of the bride took my sisters and me back to our apartment as quickly as possible. My parents were surprised to see us so early, since Afghani weddings usually go on until midnight.

Chakila wanted to know if there had been a news flash, but the radio had announced nothing in particular. The next day everything was still normal. We all went off to our separate occupations. But at around eleven, Chakila came to fetch me from school. When the teacher asked her for a reason, she simply said that it was important for me to get home. On the way, she explained, 'There may be war in Kabul. I have to warn the whole family.'

She rang Father in the store as soon as we got home. I heard her asking him to bring supplies and then come back as soon as possible. Then she rang the airport to alert Soraya and call her home as well. Chakila had a bizarre air about her. She was pretending calm, but every five minutes she leapt up to look out the window to see if our parents were on their way. An hour and a half later, we were all gathered.

'Why all this hurry?' Father asked.

'I took my usual route on the way to the newspaper office this morning, and immediately noticed that things were not right. The shops were closed. Barricades were being built out of sand bags. I saw armed men, wearing turbans, and you know that no one apart from the military is allowed to carry arms in the city. When our car arrived in front of the Ministry of Water and Electricity, near the Festival Square, a soldier signalled for us to stop. I showed him my press card and told him I was on my way to the paper. But he ordered me to turn back and said, "Gulbuddin Hekmatyar's men are here." I asked him who this Hekmatyar was and at that moment a man in traditional dress and sporting a beard and a turban started to scream, to howl – "We are the Hezb-e-Islami of Hekmatyar."

'And all of a sudden, the car was surrounded by turbanned men. I asked the taxi driver to turn round immediately. He was just doing so when the soldier who had asked me to stop hailed me again. He wanted me to take along two young female employees from the ministry. They got in and told me that these bearded men had hit them and humiliated them, and all because they were wearing skirts and tights. The men had pulled off their tights and tied them round their necks. Then they had spat in their faces and cursed them as Communists. After we had crossed the bridge back into our borough, everything was calm and it was hard to imagine that a few hundred metres away, the situation was so different.'

That night we ate around seven thirty. The fighting began soon after. Chakila ran up to Saber's apartment on the sixth floor, the better to see where the battles were taking place. Although they were forbidden at that time, Saber had a pair of binoculars. He was in love with Victoria who lived in the building opposite and he had managed somehow to find this pair of binoculars so that he could watch his beloved from his terrace. His mother, who worked in the management of the Presidential Palace, confirmed to Chakila that the bearded men in turbans had sent all the women home from work during the day, vilifying them as Communists.

That meant that Hekmatyar's men had already reached the palace. From the sixth floor windows, Chakila could see the eerie play of light cast by rockets and gunfire in the Pole Mahmoud Khan zone, just opposite the palace, as well as near the hospital and the Shashdarak Quarter next to the radio and television headquarters. Strangely, broadcasting continued as normal, though no one gave any news of the combat before our very noses.

Chakila was very nervous and kept on repeating, 'You see. You see. I was right.'

Soraya and I stuffed cushions in front of our bedroom window. I kept thinking of what the girls at school had been saying. 'If the extremists make it to Kabul, there'll be no more make-up, no more western clothes. You'll see. They won't even let us ride our bikes.'

A few minutes later, the explosions came so close that the people on the sixth and fifth floors went to take refuge in the cellar. They were most exposed to rocket fire.

For over two days the fighting went on, without the government giving us any kind of news. Finally, on the third day, Radio Kabul announced that Hekmatyar's men had been expelled from the city and their attempt at invasion repelled.

After that, came the announcement of the formation of the State of Islamic Afghanistan, under the new government of Commander Massoud, now called Master of Kabul. I can still hear the words of this declaration: 'From next Saturday, everyone and in particular women, must return to work. Girls' and boys' schools will re-open.'

Like me, my school friends were greatly relieved. Hekmatyar had made us fear for our most basic rights. We wanted the freedom to study and then to work. And so we wanted this fanatic to be pushed back as far as possible to the north and to Pakistan.

A week later, there was a TV documentary on the crimes committed by the Communists. There were pictures of groups of prisoners undergoing mass execution at the prison of Pol-e-Tcharkhi, hundreds of scattered shoes, communal graves. Under the Communist regime, thousands of people accused of anti-Communism had been arrested, executed and thrown into mass graves. Rumours were rife about Afghan political prisoners transported to Siberia.

A few months after this, my friend Anita, happy and full of hope, came to say goodbye to me. She and her mother were going off to the Soviet Union to search for her father. They had sold their house to pay for the journey. I was sad, so sad to see them go in search of a phantom. Much later, Anita came back without ever having located her father.

The atmosphere in Kabul was bizarre. On the one hand

we were still free to wander about, to study, to work; on the other we were living in the midst of daily civil war imposed by Hekmatyar and his followers.

In 1993, the battles took on intensity and were terribly violent. In winter, which is not a school season for Afghanis because it's too cold, many of Kabul's schools were turned into refugee camps for displaced families. The south, the west and the centre of the capital were under heavy fire. People fled to take refuge in the northern districts, Others left for Jalalabad or Pakistan. We were in the midst of real ethnic clashes. The Pashtuns killed the Hazars, the Hazars killed the Tajiks . . . Everyone knew that the man responsible for all this killing was still Gulbuddin Hekmatyar, who was totally dependent on the Pakistani secret services.

In order to terrorize the population, young boys carried out food poisoning operations by injecting a toxic substance into our fruit and vegetables. Those who ate them fell ill. Some even died. The inhabitants of Kabul were in panic. They didn't dare buy fresh produce from hawkers and stall keepers. After a few weeks, one of these gangs of boys was stopped and shown on television. The panic abated.

The rockets fell randomly, anywhere and everywhere. Some days we counted 300. On others, they peaked at 1,000. The hospitals were full of the wounded. Drugs were in short supply. Doctors worked night and day.

In January 1994, the troops of Gulbuddin Hekmatyar, now strengthened by those of Generals Dostom and Mazari, leaders of the Hazars, began a bloody campaign. At four o'clock in the morning on 1 January, the bombardment started. It lasted without respite for a week. With our neighbours, we all huddled in the cellar. Water and electricity had been cut off throughout the city. Then the opposing sides decided on some kind of truce that allowed foreign diplomats to leave the city. We made use of this, too, to seek refuge in the north of the capital. On the way we met thousands of people, entire families, who had had to leave their homes.

The battle lasted for over seven months. During this time much of the city was burnt down and destroyed. The university – one of the largest in the region – went up in flames. Burnt and pillaged: the university library, the second largest in Asia. Destroyed and pillaged, the museum. Somehow, despite it all, we carried on living. I went to school. My sister Chakila got married.

The sheer effort of living in wartime numbed us to the overall tragedy which was encompassing our country. That must have been what prevented us from seeing that the ultimate threat was yet to come. Its source was a secret movement of students of religion – a new militia, which by the end of 1994, having benefited from the war in Kabul, would have seized a third of the south-east of the country. We had a little over two years to make use of the strange type of freedom that persisted in our city during its time of siege.

Ramika, a little pupil of mine, takes her burqa off when she comes into my room and sits dutifully at my feet to listen to the reading of a poem by the famous Mohamad Hafez Cherazi.

The world for me was a mansion
In which I searched for knowledge
Under distant skies I loved to wander
To seize hold of every subtlety of thought
Of the variety of fruits
Which fed my philosophy.

Ramika will write this for her dictation and then recite it back to me afterwards.

She is fourteen, the age I was when the siege began, and just at the age where it's possible for the Taliban to apply one of their earliest, monstrous decrees: 'All young girls must be married.' I was told of the form this decree takes just a year ago. A woman in a building near by knocked at the door of an apartment. She was one of those scouts who looks out for young Afghani girls for the Taliban. The woman of the house answered her knock. She was alone with her three daughters and no sooner had she opened the door than some Taliban barged in behind the scout. They hit the mother until she lost consciousness and kidnapped the three girls. The scout told the neighbours that the girls were married to her sons and that she had a right to bring her daughters-in-law to live with her.

Ever since we heard that story, either Daoud or my father answers the door to strangers. One of my cousins fell into a diabolical Taliban trap. A Talib wanted her, insisted, and so threatened the family that my cousin was finally forced to marry another boy much younger than her, even though she had always stubbornly refused to marry before, just to get away from the Talib.

125

There are so many stories of this kind – horrible or simply lamentable. Young girls of my age, or Ramika's, having their lives destroyed. Tonight, I'm going to pray for the impossible return of women's freedom. I'll also watch Ramika's burqa with extra care as she makes her way along the street. I've changed. I've grown up.

6

The Kite Hunt

Father has been worrying ever since we opened our clandestine school. He doesn't say anything because he can see
that for Soraya, Daoud and I, it acts as a counter-irritant.
Even Mother has regained a little of her spirit. But Father
is prone to making sad comparisons.

'Ah, when you went to school, remember how different
it was? Remember when I took you to English lessons? Now
I watch you behaving like thieves in order to do something
for these children who will never do what you were able
to do. Times weren't easy for you, either. I know that. But
for these children . . .'

My poor father looks as if he's carrying the weight of the
entire world on his shoulders.

Since our pupils have been coming to the house every
day, life in our apartment has grown animated. My mother
participates. When we first started, we didn't want to disturb
her. Now she helps us as much as her strength allows. She
cooks for the children at lunchtime. She's happy to see them
eat. When they leave, she encourages them.

'You're doing well,' she says. 'It's a way of carrying on
the struggle.'

This change in our house also means more visits from

127

neighbours, since their children are with us. Before this, they would usually come to see Mother only if they had medical problems. Then they took fright and consultations grew further and further apart. When there wasn't any medication to give them, they ceased coming altogether. Now Mother can receive them without any fears; these women won't denounce us, because if they do, they're denouncing their children at the same time.

And their children are already so threatened! The girls, in the first instance, but the boys too. There's a hideous rumour making the rounds. Small boys have disappeared. Some have been found maimed or dead. The Taliban are using them for the black market in internal organs. That's what they say. Rumours buzz through Kabul at breakneck speed. If only we had even a single independent newspaper, like the one where Chakila worked, they would have run an investigation. But I'm dreaming. Our city is walled in, a citadel of silence where only whispers and unverifiable information circulate.

Before the Taliban came, I did work experience at Chakila's paper. I was thirteen when a group of friends and I decided to create our own youth paper. There was nothing available aimed specifically at us and we wanted to change this. We put out our homemade newspaper – Farida, Maryam, Saber and I – with a little help from my big sister. It came out every term and was called *Fager*, which means 'Dawn'. We wrote it by hand and there was a single copy that circulated from house to house, going round the school, friends and their families. It sometimes came back months later, a bit ragged, often with the photos of stars cut out . . .

On the last page, we had stuck an envelope in which our readers could send their suggestions to us. We used these to decide on topics for our next issue.

We included articles gathered from Iranian magazines that talked about women's issues, plus information about universities and careers. Lighter subjects – fashion, make-up, music – were there too. I cut out pictures of movie stars and models. We carried reviews of the latest books and CDs. I also photocopied postcards of actors from American and Indian films and told anecdotes from their lives. For more serious subjects, my sisters, particularly Chakila, helped with political and general information.

I had just about finished putting together the final issue of the year when the Taliban invaded. But I couldn't finish it. I didn't have the courage. Farida and Daoud took it over. This was my brother's way of making me believe in the project again. He would have liked me to carry on with it, but I no longer felt like it. I gave up and so did the others. Where were we to find news now that the entire press was censored and we were altogether cut off from the world? Apart from the rare letters that Daoud receives from his friends exiled in Germany, London or Holland, the little bit of news that we get from Wahid in Russia and the radio secretly listened to at night, there is nothing. The emptiness makes one delirious. Daoud says that everyone in the outside world has forgotten that Kabul exists. His friends think that there are very few Afghanis left in the capital and that we're utterly overrun with Pakistanis.

Each time that we discuss what the rest of the world's

population might think of us, he's the one who's most pessimistic.

'You think it bothers them at all? I don't think so. They don't even know where Afghanistan is. I'm sure they don't even believe in what's happening here. They have nothing to do with it. Even the Afghanis who live abroad don't give a damn!'

Twice we had the good fortune to get magazines from the Arab Emirates through a friend of Daoud's who works at Air Ariana. The airline still flies, but without any women. The only destinations are Islamabad, Dubai, Djedda and Saudi Arabia. Two magazines in three years is a pretty skimpy source of news.

It's Farida, with her gift for asking questions that already contain their own answers, who wakes us up.

'What if we took up our newspaper again? Don't you feel like it? I do. We only have to begin.'

She proposes to take a walk into town, a reporter invisible beneath her burqa, to gather information for our next issue. To help us, Daoud will take care of the paper supply, and because his handwriting is so beautiful, he'll also be responsible for the writing of it all.

We long for Chakila. Since her marriage, her authority and her smile are equally missed by everyone at home. She was the one who supervised both Soraya and my studies with great attention. She also adored music and film. It was she who convinced Father to take us to the movies. She herself was a wonderful student, because she was curious about everything. At eleven, she got the top mark in Russian in her class, which earned her a holiday in the Soviet Union and condemnation from Wahid, who refused to allow her to travel. But she held her ground.

Chakila began to work at an independent paper while she was still at university. Today I think with enthusiasm of the period I spent at that same newspaper. How lucky I was. I was only thirteen and every day, despite the rocket fire that announced the beginning of the long road to Kabul's destruction, I went off to work with my sister. In 1994, we were just beginning to understand the complexity of the differences between the various movements of the Resistance: the aborted coup d'état of 1 January, for example, when the Uzbek militias of General Dostom and the ultra-fundamentalists of Hekmatyar tried to overthrow the Tajik President Rabbani, supported by Commander Massoud's troops. Journalists baptized that episode 'The Fifth Battle of Kabul'. A million people were on the move, fleeing battles that raged through the countryside. The attempted coup d'état failed. Massoud managed to push back the fundamentalists in the capital by June. Chakila, however, predicted that we would never have peace.

'Pakistan doesn't want a strong nation, based on agreement between the Mujahidin, on its doorstep. They want us torn apart, lacking in unity. While our country is destabilized by these tribal wars, Pakistan can happily continue its aggressive policy towards India while all the time benefiting from America's financial support. American policy in Asia is a mistake from beginning to end.'

One morning when we got to the paper, the news was very bad. Mirwais Jalil, an Afghan journalist who worked for the BBC, had just been assassinated by Gulbuddin

Hekmatyar's men. That afternoon, we went to pay our respects at the hospital. We saw the mark his executioners had left on the poor man's tortured body. A foreign journalist who had been accompanying him revealed the reason for the assassination. Jalil had filmed Pakistani and Arab fighters in Hekmatyar's ranks. So Hekmatyar wanted to scare Jalil and to wipe out this evidence of foreign mercenaries amongst the extremist Afghans.

Every night, while she worked at the paper, Chakila brought us news that she picked up at work and at the university. She wrote a lot of it down in her notebook. I would listen to her passionately and I would use some of her anecdotes for our own newspaper. For example, I remember the entire case of Mrs Zarmina. It perfectly evoked the diabolic waywardness of the Communist administration.

Mrs Zarmina was a cleaner in the Department of Public Transport for the city of Kabul. She worked at Riassat Melli Bus Company. She was a courageous woman, illiterate, who had signed up as a member of the Communist Party at her work place. It was probably obligatory. To become a Party member, she would have had to take the oath of allegiance that included never lying to her superiors and never betraying the Party. One day, while she was carrying out her cleaning duties, she heard the head of the department, his deputy and several others talking. They were discussing the resale of bus parts, something that was totally illegal. The director asked his deputy to ensure that buses belonging to the state broke down more often and were declared unusable, so that they could be sent off to the garage. The engines and detachable parts were then removed and resold. The money went straight into the officials' pockets.

Having promised never to lie to the Party, Mrs Zarmina faithfully reported what she had heard to the administrative service of the Department of Transport. Present at the occasion were Farid Muzdak of the political bureau and a member of the then ruling party, Watan. Poor Mrs Zarmina had no idea she was dealing with an organized mafia. But Farid Mazdak thanked her and told her she would receive the medal of merit.

The next day, Mrs Zarmina had still not come home and her anxious husband presented himself at Riassat Melli Bus. No one knew where the woman was. After a week, her husband returned to the company with his children and insisted that his wife come back to him. He was certain that she must be somewhere in the building.

That indeed was the case. The director has been keeping her prisoner for a week. He received her husband in his office, locked the door behind him and insisted that he watch the rape of his wife. After this, he told the poor man that he only needed to divorce her if he wasn't happy and he tried to force him to sign a document demanding divorce. Completely bewildered, not knowing what to do, the husband hesitated. So the director had Mrs Zarmina's head shaved in front of her children. The husband still hesitated. Furious at such resistance, the director had the children thrown into the Kabul River, right opposite the Riassat Mellli Bus Company. Mrs Zarmina managed to escape, jumped into the water and saved her son. Unfortunately the current carried away her little girl.

Mad with pain, the poor woman went home. Her husband didn't want her any more, but she didn't give up. She needed to see all this through to the end. She went to the Ministry of Transport to complain. But General Khalil, who was also implicated in the illegal trafficking of parts, ordered his guards to punish her and chuck her out.

Mrs Zarmina's tragic case lasted over two years. Everyone took her for a mad woman. No one would believe her story. Even when she requested to see Fazel Haq Khaliqyar, the non-Communist Prime Minister of Dr Najibullah's government, he refused her an interview.

Chakila told the woman's story in her newspaper, fortunately still independent despite the threats of the Watan Party. The public feature allowed the poor woman at last to triumph over the misery and injustice she had suffered. When the Resistance took control of the capital in April 1992, the woman went to seek justice from the new masters of Kabul. The implicated mafiosi were at last stopped and imprisoned.

But then the Taliban arrived. Mrs Zarmina lost the right to work. She had to take refuge in Pakistan. According to the last reports Chakila was able to gather, she was living with her son in the refugee camp of Nasser Bagh, a few kilometres from the city of Peshawar.

Reports of rape were frequent in the newspapers of that period. Rape is still frequent under the Taliban, but the reports don't appear in the newspapers any more. Under the Communist regime, a journalist for the weekly *Saba'won* even published an article on a hideous group rape, having first taken the precaution of changing all the names because important members of the Party were implicated in the affair.

Parwin was a young woman working in the Ministry of Education. The rapists were colleagues in the Ministry who invited her to a party. When she arrived she realized that she was the only woman present. But it was too late to leave alone. They forced her to drink. A good number had collaborated in this premeditated encounter. And even the chauffeur participated in the ultimate rape. It was the guardian of the house who took Parwin to the hospital. She was unconscious. The journalist who wrote the story was at the hospital on the same day, quite by chance. Parwin had time to tell her everything before she died.

Another story that I'll never forget was told by members of Chakila's editorial team. It had to do with a child born at the maternity hospital of Malalai in Kabul who only lived for eight hours. His mother came from the region of Salang in the north of the city. The child had a frighteningly distorted face, only one eye in the middle of his forehead and an ear on the top of his head, while his mouth was on his cheek. He was both legless and armless. Some of the doctors contended that this deformed child had been produced because of the horrors of war suffered by his mother. Laboratory tests finally showed that both mother and child had been exposed to chemicals transported on Scud missiles. The Soviet army had used these chemicals for the first time in the Salang valley.

These reports date from a time when, despite civil war, we weren't condemned to a single source of information. It was a time when television functioned and newspapers appeared, when life was still possible. Radio Sharia's news these days still concerns women: now there's a prohibition on speaking in the street as the sound of our voices could 'provoke' merchants in the bazaar.

All we're left with now is the 'street radio', whispered by those who come and go with relative freedom – men. The tide of rumour takes on the status of reports. These are once more talking about that Saudi friend of the Taliban, Bin Laden, and of the marriage – past or recent, the date and location are unknown – of Mullah Omar, chief of the Taliban, with one of Bin Laden's numerous daughters. The streets report that this wedding was ostentatiously depraved. Evidently the rules of the Taliban hardly apply to their own members.

Far from this luxury, one of my old classmates, Hafezo, came to the house and proposed that she could rent books to us for five afghani pennies per volume. Her mother bakes bread for a few pennies, like many impoverished women. We were so sad for her that Daoud decided to rent a book from her for a week, even if we never read it. Daoud has a tender and silent heart, quite the opposite of our elder brother. He doesn't speak much, but he's always prepared to be of service.

In July 1998, he got married. In normal days, a wedding is a real celebration. Daoud's left us with a bitter and stormy memory. It's almost as if nothing happened and he really isn't married. Yet his wife, Marie, lives with us, as custom demands.

Daoud was eager to be married. One day a mate of his talked to him about Marie, a friend of his wife's, a young woman of good family who he thought might suit Daoud. He invited Daoud home and because Marie lived in the house next door, my brother could see her in her parents' garden. He couldn't meet her properly, as young people used to do before the days of the Taliban. That was frustrating, but nonetheless, he liked the look of her. In any case he had reached the age of twenty-nine and was determined to marry.

My parents then went to see hers, according to the rules: in Afghanistan it's always the parents who organize marriages. My grandmother used to say that love came after the nikha, the religious ceremony. Given the situation in Kabul, there was no engagement and we were all sad that the betrothed couldn't see each other. No celebration, no music, no gifts, no pretty dress. Mother often told us how for her wedding she had worn a magnificent green dress made by the official court tailor, Azar. Then, when evening came, she donned a long white dress from Paris, which the wife of the chief of information services had lent her. The green dress, colour of hope for Muslims, is the traditional one for the religious ceremony. At night, the fashion was to go western: white came to us from Europe. During the marriage vows, the bride and groom exchange rings and an old respectable female member of the family comes to put henna on the palms of their hands. After that the couple gaze into a special mirror that they will later take to their room. The newlyweds read a verse of the Koran, and share a glass of a sweet drink, so that their union will be sweet for the whole of their lives. At the end of the ceremony, a sheep is bled and if the spreading blood reaches the shoes of the bride, it means that she'll stay faithful for ever.

Absolutely none of this for Daoud and Marie . . . Yet we told ourselves that we had to do something to celebrate the occasion.

But where to go? Impossible to choose a restaurant as we had done for Chakila's wedding when a hundred guests came. No establishment would now accept men and women together. And our apartment was too small and too exposed to the neighbours' and the Taliban's curiosity. Short of hiding in a cellar, as we did in the worst of the bombardment, we couldn't think of a way to celebrate the union.

Marie's parents lived in a house with a garden in another quarter of Kabul. Their neighbours were friends of Daoud's friend. We decided to chance meeting at their place for a ceremony.

It was a long time since Soraya and I had put our noses outside. Even longer since we'd been to a wedding. But there was little excitement and no preparation. We couldn't wear make-up or buy new dresses. The guests were at a strict minimum: a few friends of Daoud's and the members of both families. My brother was miserable at not being allowed to wear a good suit and tie as these were prohibited. His friends teased him.

'It's not so bad, Daoud. In any case, there'll be no photographer, because photographs are forbidden. So no one will know you weren't in a suit.'

Seeing Daoud's despondent face, one of them got upset.

'No, this is ridiculous. I can't see my best friend married

without at least making a video so that he can have a souvenir. I'll take care of it.'

So he came with his camcorder. We started off by doing things according to Taliban rules – no mixed reunions, even for weddings. The women stayed in one room. The men in another. For the ceremony, the bride and groom had somehow to come together for the exchange of rings. The families assembled in the garden. Daoud and Marie stood next to each other. It was the most symbolic moment and Daoud's friend took out his camera, another put on a music cassette. Suddenly someone shouted, 'Taliban, Taliban. Watch it.'

Panic broke out. The friend turned off the music and hid the cassettes and player, all in a minute. Nobody knew how he had done it. But the Taliban had heard. Furious, they started to search everyone, to no effect. However, the amateur cameraman hadn't managed to hide his camcorder. They beat him up, seized his camera, threw it down on the ground and stamped on it in a rage, as if they were stamping on the devil himself. The few images of Daoud's marriage were ripped into pieces.

The guests vanished under the Taliban's smug noses. We went home with the bride in a car. We slipped away like thieves, though the custom is that even the departure from the wedding is a real ceremony. The whole thing was a disaster.

Luckily, my brother's camera-carrying friend wasn't seriously injured, but, of course, his camera was destroyed. The rest of us were in a state of shock. Father was furious, Soraya in tears, Daoud disgusted. It was shameful for him to bring a bride home in such lamentable conditions. Traditionally, we honour the marriage of a son with major celebrations. Welcoming a new member into the bosom of the family is meant to be an occasion of happiness and joy. (When a daughter leaves, it's not the same. The joy is meant to be on the side of the groom's family.)

Poor Daoud, to have this important moment utterly ruined and to be humiliated by two or three Taliban wanting to show off their power. What exactly are they looking for by depriving an entire population of holidays and pleasure, of family memories? The answer I always arrive at is horribly simple. They want to stop us living – exterminate us, slowly but surely, for their own benefit.

There are no more kites in the skies of Kabul. We used to see dozens of them floating above the city. Young boys would climb up on the roofs of buildings to catch the wind, daring a possible fall as they kept their eyes on the skies. They often did tumble. Every year, the hospitals took in boys injured by kite flying. But their beautiful, multi-coloured paper birds were a symbol of our skies.

Children who didn't have enough money to buy kites manufactured something called a chelak – a treacherous instrument composed of a stone tied to the end of a string. Armed with this, off they went to look out other boys' kites. When they found one they particularly wanted, they launched their missile into the kite's path. If the two strings got tangled, the little thieves had only to wait for their booty to hit the ground and off they would run with a new kite.

The hunt for kites often ended up in fights. These were

even fiercer when the 'kite hunters' used a superior chelak equipped with two stones and much surer in aim. It wasn't only petty thieves who engaged in kite hunting. Boys like Daoud, who couldn't quite manage the difficult business of flying their own kites, treated the hunt itself as a game.

One evening, to make me laugh, Soraya tells me the story of the kite that fell right on top of Daoud when he was little. It happened in our old house, before I was even born.

'Daoud was playing with his chelak in the garden when suddenly a neighbour's chelak missed its target and hit Daoud on the head, followed by a kite. He was injured, bleeding from the mouth, and he didn't dare go into the house for fear of being reprimanded. His friend Abdullah took him to his mother's instead. They rented the first floor of the house and she was a nurse. She stitched up his head and took him home. An hour later, it was Abdullah's turn. He fell off the roof with his kite. His knee was bleeding and his mother rushed up to ours screaming that her son was hurt. This time it was our mother who provided the stitches and the dressing.'

Daoud had calmed down by the time I was born. He hardly ever fought any more and he was a serious student who got good grades, particularly in maths. He loved the movies. He also had a wonderful collection of miniature cars and he bought a new one every month.

Mother still often tells us the story of her sons' circumcision, which had to be carried out for the two of them together. There was a big celebration with over a hundred guests. She had had white suits made for the boys. A large sheep was killed and garlands of light bulbs had been strung throughout the courtyard of the house. Circumcision is usually carried out by a barber, but Mother chose a doctor. Father had carefully explained to his sons what was going to take place. For my elder brother, everything happened as foreseen. But little Daoud was very frightened when his turn came. As is the habit on these occasions, the doctor said to him, 'Look up at the sky, little one . . .'

Taut with apprehension, Daoud answered, 'Get on with it. Cut it off. I know what you're going to do.'

Wahid and Daoud were always embarrassed when Mother or our aunts repeated this story. They grumbled. The stories weren't funny to them, they said. Nor had it been their celebration; they had had to suffer while everyone else had fun.

Wahid was always a fighter and he enlisted. Daoud wanted nothing more than to avoid it. He went on with his education at the Omar Shahid senior school. In the winter of 1987, when Daoud was eighteen and had just taken his finals, he went out one morning to get his results. When he didn't return by nightfall, the entire family grew worried. Father went out to do the rounds of the neighbourhood and find out if any of Daoud's friends had seen him. Meanwhile Chakila phoned Wahid at his barracks. Wahid told her that he would take care of it. Towards midnight, a military truck stopped in front of the house. Wahid, in uniform, stepped out of it with a trembling Daoud just behind.

I never witnessed the scene because I was too little, but I've had it told to me so many times I have the impression

I was right there. Wahid lectured Daoud, told him he was not to leave the house, then went back to his barracks. We all listened as Daoud told us what had happened.

'We had been told to stand in front of the school until our results were announced. After about two hours, we were ushered into the courtyard. Suddenly soldiers encircled the building and officers burst into the yard. They turned the main hall into a recruiting office. They told us they were calling students up in alphabetical order in order to direct them towards different army units. All of my class were destined for the Gardez regiment in the south. Those with friends in high places started to telephone. In less than an hour they left for home. But my friends and I didn't know what to do, whom to call. Everyone was frightened of ending up on the Front, Kalashnikov in hand, like Wahid. They're not supposed to conscript us until our studies are finished. After all, we pay for our studies. Anyhow, that's when I saw Wahid arrive in his presidential guard uniform with six soldiers behind him. He was in a rage. The soldiers in the room saluted him and he sent them to find the school principal and find him quickly. When the man arrived, he said to him in no uncertain terms, "What you're doing here is illegal. You have no right to keep the students here without alerting their parents." The recruitment officer retorted that he was only obeying instructions. Wahid radioed the recruitment centre and explained the situation to the permanent officer in charge. He was told that the students had indeed to be let go. All my friends rushed off and Wahid took me home.'

All this happened during the Soviet occupation when

143

young people were persuaded to enlist in the Afghan army. Some, like my elder brother, had freely chosen to do so, because after all military service was obligatory. But Daoud was only eighteen and Wahid was altogether opposed to his little brother going through what he, himself, had experienced. He knew that Daoud detested the military and war, and if he had had to fight the Resistance from the midst of a Soviet-led battalion, he couldn't have put up with it.

For three months, Daoud lived more or less in hiding at home while waiting for the university entrance exam. During this time, Chakila was charged with running errands for him. She would take me to hire video cassettes for him, because he needed distraction if he were really to be kept in the house. It wasn't easy. He'd pace the apartment like a bear trapped in a cage. In our building alone, six other young men were in the same situation as he was. They would get together in the halls at the end of the day to chat.

One evening while I was playing with my sisters in front of the building, Malek Raihan, a neighbour, came running to tell us to alert Daoud that an army patrol was in the neighbourhood. I ran to warn my brother and his friends and they hurried into their own apartments, where hiding places had been prepared just in case. My mother was furious with Daoud that day and she laid down the law: he was not to leave the apartment. He was even kept home during two family wedding celebrations.

It was a time when even our folksongs and popular songs

recorded the matter of military service. At weddings women sang,

> The wind blows and carries away my headscarf
> Just as the patrol has carried away my loved one.
> May God carry away these patrols
> Who carried away my faithful loved one.

All kinds of stories circulated on this subject. One of our neighbours told us that in the Parwan district, while soldiers were searching houses for young men, they went into one where the parents told them that their son had just died. It was a trick. Their son was only lying on his bed, pretending. But a few minutes later it turned out to be true: their son really was dead.

There were hundreds of stories like this making the rounds of Kabul. Each household had its own to tell. Within one family, some members might be on the side of the Resistance, while others were on the government side. Families were torn apart. The questions were so difficult to resolve: to be Afghan and fight with the Afghan army led by Soviets against other Afghans? To be a pro-Communist or anti-Communist Afghan? To stay neutral? All this was trebly difficult when a son arrived at conscription age, an age that kept on changing depending on the whims of the government and the needs of the army.

During one birthday celebration evening, the guests started to sing in our traditional quatrains. There were families who came from Kohestan, which extends some fifty kilometres to the north of Kabul, and others from the city itself. The lyrics they chose revealed their political affiliation and largely separated country from city. The pro-Communist city-dwellers sang,

> Oh! The brave, proud young man
> Erect on his tank, he rolls towards the Front,
> Erect on his tank, he moves towards the battle
>   at Panshir
> While all the women weep behind him.

Meanwhile, the Resistance supporters from Kohestan sang,

> I was in a field of flowers when a Mujahidin called
> With great kindness, he offered me tea,
> My thanks go to him, but he should keep his tea
>   for himself.
> I adore him with his rifle on his shoulder.

At the end of the winter, the press announced that young people could now come and enrol at the university and present themselves for the competitive entrance exams. The military patrols went out that day as usual to carry out their raids on the city and interrogate the students. The checkpoints had become more and more numerous and well-defended.

Wahid took Daoud and a few other young men from the neighbourhood to the university in his own jeep because army jeeps weren't stopped by the patrols. But that wasn't enough. During the examinations, the boys' papers were graded far more severely than the girls. The government did everything it could to ensure that this selection process gave them the largest possible number of young males.

All day we waited in apprehension. Daoud finally came home at the end of the afternoon. He looked satisfied. He had reason to feel optimistic because he always came second in his high school class. He had chosen to do economics and had passed the entrance exam.

At that time, once a student was enrolled at university, he received a student card and an official dispensation from the army certifying that his military service was postponed. This authorisation was good for three months. Exams took place at the end of every term, which was three months long. After each exam, the certificate was renewed if the student had done well, annulled in the case of failure.

The first term, Daoud got the top mark in his class. This should have earned him a scholarship to continue his studies in the Soviet Union. He didn't want to go but Father preferred him to leave Kabul in order to escape the army's clutches. However, because he wasn't a Communist Party member, the scholarship wasn't granted. Daoud rowed with the secretary of the Communist Youth organization who was responsible for granting the subsidies. The only answer he got was, 'There isn't one for you.'

Finally my father intervened personally with the secretary. He insisted and made such a public fuss about the injustice done to Daoud, that the scholarship finally came. It was, however, valid only in Dushanbe in the Republic of Tajikistan and not in Moscow. Daoud accepted it nonetheless and he went off to do his economics studies in Dushanbe.

147

It was a good thing that he did because the rules concerning conscription changed with no forewarning. From one day to the next, students had to carry out six months of military service – whether they were sons of ministers or simple citizens. The government had decided that given the needs of the moment, every male had to do two years of service. Luckily Daoud was in Tajikistan.

We corresponded with him. From time to time he phoned home. After a year, he came back to Kabul for holidays and told us about the poverty and misery he had seen in Dushanbe. Soviet administrators here never stopped telling us wonderful things about the Soviet people, whereas in fact many of them lived in terrible conditions.

'I met a woman who worked in a state farm for two rubles a day,' Daoud told us. 'The professors there give you a good grade in exchange for a mere key-ring. A pair of jeans sold in Dushanbe will pay your university costs for a whole year. All the Afghan students arrived with jeans, sunglasses, umbrellas. Anything really that you can find in Peshawar is worth a fortune there. Even a pair of nail clippers or a packet of chewing gum.'

In the student milieu in Tajikistan, Daoud said, the fashion was Soviet.

'The richest men marry Russian women and give their children Russian first names like Natasha, Treshkova, Valentina, Alexis, Ivan. That's part of the Sovietization programme. Young Tajiks go to Moscow and Russians come to fill their places.'

He also told us that the Sovietization of Tajikistan had brought with it a national identity problem for the Tajiks, even though they acquired their independence from Moscow in 1991.

The following holidays, in August 1992, Daoud came back to a Kabul that no longer had a Communist government. It had fallen in April to the pressure of the Mujahidin alliance. But the fundamentalist Hekmatyar was still waiting for power. He never stopped raining rockets on Kabul.

That holiday month was a difficult one for Daoud. He'd lost the habit of living amidst rocket fire. He couldn't understand why we weren't frightened. For him, it seemed terrible. But we'd grown used to it.

We inhabited the eastern room of our apartment in order to avoid being in the line of fire. One day at about one o'clock, we had just finished our lunch and were watching television with our tea, when two rockets landed just opposite our building. We always left the windows open so that they wouldn't break. We saved them that time too, but our neighbours' windows were all pulverized.

We ran for shelter in the hall of the building, the only place that was protected from the splintering glass. Daoud and I were both crying. The explosions had ignited a fire nearby and already the building was beginning to burn. We threw buckets of water everywhere to extinguish the flames and we had just about managed to do so when Wahid arrived. He had gone down into the street at the first burst of fire.

'Is everyone all right?'

Beside themselves, Mother and Daoud shouted, 'Where were you? What are you doing outside at a time like this?'

'It's war. I went out to help the neighbours. All the men

went down to put out the fire. There are wounded. One dead, too.'

One of our neighbours, who had just got married, had been hit in the kidneys and died.

When we returned to the room we had been in at the start of the explosions, the mosquito net on the window had some ten shell holes in it.

The Mujahidin units in our quarter had helped people to put out the fire and had transported the wounded to the hospital. Two hours later, the electricity was cut. We listened to the news on the transistor radio: over a hundred rockets had fallen in the course of the day. Some twenty people were dead. One hundred and fifty were injured.

Daoud, who had his ears glued to the radio, said, 'I'm going to leave Kabul. I want to finish my studies.'

The very next day he went to the Ministry of Foreign Affairs, despite the fighting. He got his travel visa, a plane ticket, and a week later, he flew off to Dushanbe, via Tashkent. When he had left for his holidays, he had been told the new Afghan government loathed the Soviet Union and that the Kabul authorities wouldn't let him return to Tajikistan. He wasn't the only Afghan student in this situation. But the Ministry of Foreign Affairs put no difficulties in his path, so long as his fees were covered in advance by the Soviets.

Daoud stayed in Dushanbe until the autumn of 1992. When he returned home, he was twenty-three years old. The forces of Commander Massoud were still in control of Kabul. But Hekmatyar's fundamentalists, who wanted to seize power, were about to make us endure an insufferable civil war in which our daily lives never ceased to be punctuated by rocket fire.

There was no longer any question of boys climbing on roofs, their nose to the wind and eyes to the sky in search of kites. There still isn't: the Taliban have outlawed the skies as far as the little boys of Kabul are concerned. One day the prohibition will extend to the birds.

We've been at war for twenty years and it's almost four since we've been imprisoned in this house. I'll be twenty in the year 2000. Will the war still be raging? Daoud's friends say in their letters that the world has forgotten us, that we live in a pit, that the Taliban have succeed in their enterprise and that there are more and more Pakistanis in their military training camps.

The BBC says that the Americans bombed some of these camps as a reprisal for an attack on their embassies in Africa.

But the permanent attack on Afghani men and women doesn't seem to worry the Americans.

The BBC also said that opium was an important resource for the Taliban government, which taxes the traffickers at the rate of 20 per cent on their cargos.

Our country is in the hands of organized criminals. At the beginning Father always gave us hope. 'In two weeks,' he said. 'In three months . . . In six months . . .'

Now, we ask, 'How many years?'

I think of the thousands of Talibs now growing up around us.

Poor little Afghans. Poor country. The billowing kites suited it so well.

151

7

Who Speaks in Afghanistan?

Turning the knob on the transistor, we find ourselves listening to Radio Sharia: it sends shivers up our spine. Their logic fills us with dread. To deprive someone of freedom is an injustice. Therefore, to chop off the hand of a thief is a punishment far more charitable than prison. He can go back to work that way, support his family. If tomorrow in the streets of Kabul, a child steals bread from a stall because his widowed mother has no male protection, is forbidden to work and therefore condemned to begging, whose hand should the Taliban chop off?

There are thieves and thieves. According to one Taliban decree, a thief is also a man who dares to change 'small afghani notes into larger ones'. What is the guilt of this particular thief? Of lightening his pockets of the burden of inflation? Of hiding his savings from other thieves?

The 'street radio', which is what we call our active rumour mill, says that Mullah Omar always moves around with trunks full of Afghani notes, Pakistani rupees, and US dollars. No one knows if this is supposed to be the State Treasury or his own. The Taliban State is not our Afghanistan. Their Islamic Emirate has nothing to do with our Islam.

The BBC and the Voice of America rarely talk about our country these days. Daoud is right. We're like rats in some deep hole that is inaccessible to the rest of the world. However, in August 1999, we do hear that the troops of Commander Massoud have launched an offensive which has pushed the Taliban back from the plane of Shamali to the north of Kabul.

Daoud has a fatalistic thought. 'As long as the world doesn't understand that the Taliban equals Pakistan, we'll never get out of this. Everyone backs Pakistan. And so what can an isolated Mujahidin like Massoud do? Permanent civil war is no solution. There is no solution – except for exile.'

I think of my brother Wahid who's living in Moscow. He's told us about his marriage to a young Russian woman, Natasha, which took place on 1 April 2000. Yet another wedding we didn't attend.

What side would he have chosen if my parents hadn't advised him on exile? When the Taliban arrived in Kabul, some of the inhabitants saw them as saviours who would bring peace to our country, who would end the destruction of Kabul trapped amidst the gunfire of opposing rebel factions. The Taliban, they thought, would re-establish the rules of Islam. Would my brother, Wahid, have believed this too?

It's true that the rockets don't rain on us any more. Instead the city is buried in a silence that resembles death. The pro-Taliban citizens must have felt cheated from the very first day. They'd never have thought that peace would mean being deprived of all our customs – our tambourines and songs, our wedding dances and kites, our games with pigeons that were immediately prohibited on pain of the pigeons' throats being slit. Another decree.

The street radio tells us – but is it true? – that Mullah Omar is frightened of Kabul, which is why he lives in Kandahar in a house built for him by his father-in-law, Bin Laden. Meanwhile Radio Sharia tells us that this Bin Laden now proposes to support the financing and supply of the Kabul bakeries, which the UN had previously done.

When the UN Security Council imposed sanctions on the Taliban at the end of 1999 because they refused to extradite Bin Laden to the United States, where he was accused of terrorism, he answered with a threat: 'You will suffer the earthquakes and tornadoes of God; you'll be surprised by what happens to you.'

In 1996 I learned during one of the modules for my journalism course that the unknown Mr Bin Laden financed mosques. Mosques and bread are the two pillars of life in Kabul. That's why he's taken on such importance in our country. I wonder what he'll finance next. I'd like to be able to do an illustrated piece on Bin Laden in the next issue of our paper, *Fager*, but that's impossible. No portraits of him are available in Kabul, no images, since these aren't allowed.

The gathering of interesting information for our newspaper presents us with several problems. Farida brings back rumours from the street merchants. Daoud hears the whispers in the shops. But subjects are rare in this city in the year 2000 which the rest of the world will celebrate. We used to celebrate the New Year too, but the Taliban decided this was a pagan practice. Are flowers pagan? Is Soraya with her postcard flower collection at fault?

The year 2000 brought no news for our paper . . . except *Titanic*. Yes, *Titanic*. *Fager 2000* was blessed with a rather pagan windfall. Daoud brought us a poster of Leonardo DiCaprio. He even managed to find a cassette of the film that had come from Pakistan. The stalls are selling *Titanic* knick-knacks in the Kabul river bed that drought has transformed into a bazaar, as is often the case.

The black market is agog with *Titanic*. The *Titanic* style is the height of fashion everywhere, especially at the barbers. Radio Sharia announced that twenty-eight barbers had been stopped and condemned for having cut the hair of young men in the style of Leonardo DiCaprio.

Tape machines and television sets are whirring in the cellars of Kabul residents. People make their rebellions as and where they can. There are no arms, after all, in the city. Women can only walk with their heads bent. Men's backs arch under the lash of whips. But secretly, rebelliously, we delight in the passionate story of the *Titanic* lovers and we weep over the death of Leonardo amidst the ice floes of the Atlantic.

This may seem terribly superficial, given that our daily life is so horrible. The country is starving to death. Refugees from the countryside mass in camps at the border of Pakistan and Iran. Beggar women grow in number in the streets of Kandahar, Kabul, Herat, Mazar-e-Sharif and Jalalabad. But the Taliban talk of none of this. They're too busy putting barbers in prison, whipping men or punishing women. So, since decrees forbid both women and men to laugh in the streets and adolescents to play, we resist the government by weeping over the story of a pagan love.

Leonardo is so beautiful. The young girls in my neighbourhood lust after him as they look at his picture. I glue his photo into *Fager* with the sensation that I'm rebelling in the way only a twenty-year-old can, a twenty-year-old who's deprived of education, of knowledge, of life.

Finally, the special *Titanic* issue is done. Daoud has illuminated the title page with his calligraphic handwriting. I don't yet know that this is going to be our last homemade newspaper.

The first of January 2001 begins sadly. We still live under the oppressive law of the Taliban. But the colour photograph of Wahid's wedding arrives to cheer us up. It has travelled through many messengers and many months. My brother is in a suit and tie, a white flower at his buttonhole. His bride, prettily made up, is wearing a white, low-cut lace dress that leaves her shoulders bare. Her blonde hair is pulled back in a chignon and covered in a delicate white veil. They both look beautiful. On the back of the photo, Wahid has written, 'Dear Mother. This is for you. The photo of our union.'

Wahid looks so happy. Where he lives, no Talib has come to break his camera. His young wife doesn't risk being whipped for having unveiled her beauty. They're free and we're in prison.

The Taliban occupy almost all our country. Winter is here. Afghans flee the cold and the famine. Daoud tells us that the Pakistani police demand money from all Afghans who want to cross the border, even from the poor devils who are fleeing famine.

The Pakistanis want our obliteration and they're not far

from getting it. Our isolation is total. The Taliban have long since ordered the closure of the special mission office of the UN in Kabul. They've excluded us from the international scene. Our nightmare will never end. The BBC has been talking of the massacre of civilians in several Taliban-occupied cities.

The Voice of America is worried about the Buddhas of Bamiyan, an archaeological marvel so famous in Afghanistan that the Buddhas appear as icons on the Air Ariana flight tickets. Daoud has them before his eyes every day at the counter where he works. These Buddhas have been the pride of the Hazaradjat region for centuries. The Taliban have already destroyed our other art treasures. They set to work early on the Kabul art museum and the frescos of Behzad, the famous Persian painter of the fifteenth century, in Herat, the city founded by Alexander the Great in the fourth century BC and capital of the Mongol Tamburlaine. Now it's the Buddhas. Even the British and the Russians respected our rich cultural heritage. Tourists used to flock to Bamiyan and Herat.

Radio Sharia announces that in conformity with the decree of the Mullah Omar ordering the destruction of all statues that predate Islam, the Buddhas of Bamiyan will be destroyed.

The Voice of America broadcasts an interview with a respected member of the international archaeological community who is indignant about the destruction of these colossal figures from the fifth century that belong to the global heritage of humanity. They also broadcast an interview with Mullah Omar's representative, who justifies the

157

demolition of the statues on the ground that they represent the gods of infidels. 'The Islamic Emirate of Afghanistan cannot tolerate such idols. These statues represent no Islamic belief. We are only breaking stones.'

In another Voice of America broadcast, Mullah Omar's representative declares that he can't confirm whether or not the Buddhas have yet been destroyed. He allows speculation that the rebels of the Northern Alliance got to the Buddhas before the Taliban did. Then he lays claim to the cultural attack.

At Bamiyan the people know who did it. They saw the Taliban machine-gunning the two colossi and launching rockets at them as they nested in the shelter of the caves they had inhabited for fifteen centuries.

According to the BBC, the entire world is shocked by the Taliban's vandalism. The only thing to equal it would be the destruction of an Egyptian pyramid.

Air Ariana tickets, however, haven't been reprinted. They still feature the Buddhas of Bamiyan.

The worst news on the BBC in this month of February 2001 is the announcement of a visit by the Minister for Health, the Mullah Mohammed Abbas, to Paris for a discussion of humanitarian issues. Radio Sharia exults over this official trip. According to the presenter, it marks a direct confirmation of the recognition by France of the Taliban State.

A Taliban in Paris, home of the rights of man! A minister of 'health' who forbids women to use hospitals, who dared in 1997 to imprison the European Commissioner for

Human Rights. Mrs Bonino had come to Kabul to look into an NGO's urgent need for funding. She was mistreated, beaten in front of a foreign cameraman who was accompanying her, and interrogated for hours before she was finally released. What right can this Talib possibly have to go abroad to discuss humanitarian questions? Everyone knows that our refugee camps are in dire straits, that drought and weather and the uninterrupted attacks of the Taliban, particularly in the north, deprive these poor refugees of everything.

Farida, Soraya and I are both furious and disgusted. The French would have done far better to invite one of our women doctors or nurses to whom work is forbidden, and who, ironically, before the Taliban regime made up the very structure of our hospitals and our heath ministry. These are the people who ran our crèches and who were indispensable to the health programme in the countryside. Through their efforts, best practice for maternal and infantile health was spread. And on top of it all, they undertook emergency gynaecological care. To send an uneducated mullah, a puppet of Pakistan who knows nothing about medicine, to France instead of one of them is a scandal.

Mother has been laid low by this new blow. This Talib has been received not only by the French Minister of Foreign Affairs, but by the President of the National Assembly. At home, we discuss the matter with unabated rage. We feel as though our trough of despair has been dug even deeper. If France can officially receive a member of the Taliban, that means that their propaganda has begun to bite abroad.

'They never invited a member of the Resistance. They

never sent a journalist to denounce what's going on in Kabul. And now they're receiving a Talib. We've had it,' Mother says.

During this time, two Afghan women declared guilty of adultery are executed in the Kabul Stadium. Ten unfaithful husbands are whipped. And in Faisalabad, in the south of Pakistan, there's an earthquake. The tremors are felt all the way to Kabul and provoke some panic.

I sometimes think that in Afghanistan we know earth-quakes rather better than the Taliban know the Koran.

April 2001. The Voice of America and the BBC announce the arrival in Paris of Commander Ahmed Shah Massoud, chief of the Resistance of Panshir.

The street radio, through its presenter Farida who's always in the information epicentre, says that Kabulis are in a state of hyper-excitement, so excited that people have been seen publicly listening to their transistor radios, having turned them up as loud as possible. This is totally prohibited. When a Talib presents himself with his censoring whip, the culprit merely retorts, 'But there's no music. I'm not listening to Iranian radio. This is only the news on Radio Sharia.'

At moments like this, a kind of madness overtakes fear. What can you expect? Paris has received an Afghan, a member of the Resistance. Kabulis are jubilant. But will Paris listen to him?

At first, Radio Sharia negates the news completely. 'Massoud isn't in Paris. It's all trickery.' Then, realising that all the prohibited radio stations are talking of nothing else – and they know that we all listen secretly every night – the Taliban turn the event to their benefit. 'The rebel has been to France solely to beg arms, in the hope that he can return with some. But even with French arms, we'll beat him.'

The 'rebel' is received by the French Ministry of Foreign Affairs, then invited as a kind of ambassador to the European Parliament. A tiny window has appeared in the Taliban-imposed walls. To say that we're filled with hope would be to speak too soon. Like all Kabulis, we're glued to the BBC, but unfortunately it gives us only the briefest of news. Massoud had a long session with the French Minister, Hubert Vedrine. He addressed the European Parliament in Strasbourg, and asked that Europe send emissaries to determine the true humanitarian situation in Afghanistan and investigate human rights abuses.

Almost at the same moment, Dr Sima, who has set up his clandestine surgery in Kabul, sends a message to Mother.

'We're looking for women who could go to Paris to talk about the situation in Afghanistan. A French Magazine together with a French association want to start up an information campaign. I can't go. There's too much need of me here. So I've told the French to contact you. It would be good if Latifa went. She could talk about our oppressed women and our clandestine schools. Witnessing is the only form of resistance we now have. And you should go with her. You were a doctor. You're my friend. And you no longer practice because of the Taliban. Go together! It's important. You'll meet the French journalists first. The magazine is called *Elle* and it's very well known. They'll arrange for you to speak to the European Parliament. You'll meet influential people, like Mrs Nicole Fontaine. We have to take this opportunity.'

I want to do it. But I'm frightened. Not only have I never travelled abroad, never taken a plane, but since my sixteenth birthday, I've lived a completely cloistered life. Why has Dr Sima chosen me? We're not the only ones, with Farida and Maryam, to run a clandestine school.

Although she's always tired and still ill, Mother wants us to go.

'Dr Sima is right,' she says. 'It's important for westerners to know that women medics are condemned to staying at home and can do nothing at all for the sick.'

Soraya, too, is all for it. 'Listen, Latifa,' she says, 'life is hard. If this could bring us any kind of change . . . You'll meet important people. Dr Sima said so.'

My father is altogether agreed. He recognizes the importance of sending out witnesses to our situation. But he's divided on practical matters. He'll have to accompany us, because we need a mahram armed with a passport in order to travel. On the other hand, he's worried about leaving Daoud at home with his wife and Soraya.

'The security of the family is a problem. If the Taliban learn of the trip while one part of the family is in Paris, the other in Kabul, we're running a serious risk of being separated for good. It's a dangerous situation.'

But the decision is finally made. Mother, Father and I are going to go, together with another young woman, Diba, who also runs a clandestine school. One of her cousins will accompany her with his passport as far as Islamabad.

The trip is organized very quickly. We'll take a minibus to Peshawar. Our visas for Pakistan are still good because we recently made a second medical trip for Mother.

On 28 April at 5.00 a.m., the taxi waits for us outside the building in order to take us to the station in good time. Diba and her cousin will join us in Pakistan; they still have to sort out a visa and passport problem.

Officially we're going to Pakistan, like the last time, in order to get medical care for Mother. To leave Daoud and Marie and Soraya, their eyes brimming with tears, in the prison of Kabul is very difficult. The journey won't be easy either. The fear of being sent back or stopped for no reason is all the greater this time because we have a secret and distant destination. Nothing we carry indicates that, of course. The instructions are simple: we have to get to Peshawar, then Islamabad and once in the capital, make contact with the Afghani Embassy in Paris by telephone. Someone will tell us where to collect our prepaid tickets. Then we go to the French Embassy in Islamabad to obtain our French visas. Finally, if that goes well, we'll take an Arab Emirates flight, which stops over in Dubai on its way to Paris.

At the border crossing, my stomach is in knots. We have a three-quarter-hour wait. The Pakistanis are making all the Hazari passengers in a minibus in front of us get off and only after some time do they allow them through. We follow.

Once we're across the border, we climb back into our vehicle and drive to Peshawar where we check into a hotel for a night. I don't know how Diba's cousin managed to get their papers in order so quickly, but they meet us in time for our departure.

I have to phone the Afghani Embassy in Paris. The telephone number is on a scrap of paper. The person who

answers me is cautious. She doesn't speak clearly, uses mean-
ingless phrases, asks who I am and if everyone else is there
. . . She tells me she'll call back tomorrow. I have the feeling
that they're checking our identity in case the call is being
monitored and overheard. I hang up and we wait.

The next day, the response is clear.

'You can go ahead. Make a note of the agency and address
and the ticket numbers. They're waiting for you.'

The road to Islamabad takes three hours. I don't know
the Pakistani capital at all, but I haven't the heart for
tourism. This adventure feels so enormous to me that I'm
filled in equal measure with anticipation and dread.

A first problem is that the man at the travel agency looks
with astonishment at our ticket numbers. 'These numbers
are wrong. There are no reservations in these numbers.'

We leave with mounting anxiety. What if all this was a
trap or another way of proving our identity? I have no idea.
I have to phone Paris and find an explanation.

'Sorry,' the woman mumbles. 'I gave you the wrong
numbers. It's a mistake. Just take these down now.'

This time, when we go to the agency, we leave with the
tickets in our hands. The next step is to obtain our visas
from the French Embassy. When we get there, we're taken
aback by the number of people who are queuing. How to
find a way through?

I stop a guard and speak to him in Pakistani. He tells
me we'll have to make an appointment. So I find another
one in front of the Embassy doors and address him in
English. 'I have to see someone in the Embassy.'

He seems to understand straight away. 'Yes. Someone's

waiting to see you. You have an appointment. You can go through.' The man walks ahead of us. He talks to someone then phones through to announce us. A few minutes later, we find ourselves in the office of a Frenchman who counts us with a hint of surprise. He talks in English with Diba's cousin, who speaks English better than I do, but I understand what they're saying.

'There are five of you, but only four who are travelling. Why is there an extra person? No one forewarned me.'

'I'm not travelling, sir. I'm only here to accompany my cousin.'

Reassured, the French man hands us some visa forms to fill out. 'You don't have to fill it all in. Only put down the essentials. How long will you be in France?'

'A week. Ten days might be better.'

In a few minutes, we have our French visas in hand. The people outside will have to wait for at least a month. It's doubly rare to get four at the same time.

The man says goodbye politely and wishes us a good trip.

We've crossed the first hurdle. The second takes place at the airport of Islamabad. Diba's cousin says goodbye. We make our way through the departure formalities and present ourselves at passport control.

The policeman looks at us strangely. My stomach sinks.

'That's odd,' he says. 'Two passports and four visas. Now why's that? How did you manage to get these visas? It's odd for the French Embassy to authorize four visas like this . . .'

We have our answer ready. 'We're going to see some

young Afghani women in France. This man is my father. He's accompanying us.'

'What young Aghani women? Why? Explain all this to me clearly. What are you going to do with those young women?'

'It's an organization for young Afghani women. My father is accompanying us.'

He raises his eyebrows and goes in search of someone. I'm terrified that he'll search our bags and find our burqas. It would be the proof that we've come from Afghanistan. We had to wear them before the border-crossing and we have to keep them for our return journey. In front of us, some young women have been turned back because of this already. If the guard finds out, too bad. I'll tell him that we usually wear them, but that he can keep them if he wants.

I look around for someone who might be able to help. Anyone. There's a man in airport uniform not far from us and I address him timidly. 'Excuse me, sir, it's my first trip. You're my father's age . . . You couldn't possibly tell this policeman not to give us too hard a time?'

'I'll go and see. He can be a real pest, that one.'

He goes to talk to the policeman who's arguing with another a little further away. While they're debating, a passenger says to my father, 'That one only wants money.'

My father takes his usual stance. 'I won't pay. I haven't any money. I can't give him anything. If he doesn't want us to go, we won't.'

The airport attendant comes back with the policemen and points me out in kindly fashion. 'Look at her. Let her go. What harm can she do? She's young. She's like my daughter. Let her be.'

The policeman hands back the passport and our visas. We can cross the barrier now, but Father keeps looking back at the official who in turn continues to watch us with an evil eye. I turn my back on him so as to stop worrying.

Father now reassures us. 'Don't worry. Our papers are perfectly in order. Everything's in order. He can't do anything.'

An hour's wait with this man's eyes on us feels like a very long time. He seems to be trying to come up with a scheme that will call us back.

Finally, we're allowed through into the boarding lounge. We're deeply relieved. There's a restaurant and toilets. We drink some tea, while Diba goes off to freshen up.

I've been keeping an eye on Mother. In fact all my thoughts are focused on her. I just hope that the trip and the tension of it won't exhaust her utterly.

The Paris flight is announced. A bus waits for us on the tarmac. There's still a distance to cross with the Pakistani sky above our heads and all the strain it breeds in us. Until the plane is airborne, I'll be frightened. In fact even while we're waiting for the plane to lift off, my fear doesn't abate. A kind of vertigo has taken me over. My head spins while the motors roar into action. I feel very weak.

Our seats are in the centre aisle and I tell myself that's all the better. I don't even want to see Pakistan from above. All I want to think about is that we're on our way to Dubai, and then to Paris.

167

The stop-over in Dubai is ghastly. All the passengers get back on the plane and we're still standing there, while a guard scrupulously examines our papers. 'You. Stand aside. Wait over there.'

We wait. We watch the passengers file through and everything starts afresh. I'm told to ring the French Embassy here. But that isn't reasonable, I protest. Finally I do, only to say that I don't know whether we'll be able to leave Dubai.

Mother rehearses with me what I have to say now if I'm interrogated. 'We're going to Paris to get medical help for my mother.'

The policeman stares at me, his face stern.

'Where are the medical papers?'

'In our luggage, on board the plane.'

'What doctor are you going to see?

'We don't know yet.'

'How can that be? You don't know anyone over there? It's your first trip. There are no other stamps in your passport. On this passport, there is no profession listed for your father. How have you managed to pay your fares?'

'We sold our house so that we could get medical help for my mother.'

'You sold your house? So that means you're not coming back?'

'Of course we're coming back. If we were leaving for good, we would have taken all our things. But we've only got a week's worth of clothes in our luggage.'

'And you've got money to pay for these medical consultations?'

'My father has four hundred dollars and some Pakistani rupees.'

'And if you run out of money?'

'My father will send for more from Pakistan.'

He counts the bills we hand him. 'Just stay here. I don't understand any of it. This visa is bizarre.'

There are only a Japanese man and ourselves left. Another policeman turns up and I repeat what I've said. He goes off to telephone someone, I don't know whom, and when he comes back, he says, 'Go on. You can go through.'

When the plane takes off for Paris, I crumble in my seat. I refuse to let myself think about what our return will be like.

In Paris, everything is simple. A man is waiting for us. He is the Charge d'Affaires at the Embassy. He introduces the French people who have organized our trip: Marie-Françoise and Catherine from the magazine *Elle*; Chékéba, President of the Free Afghanistan Association, who will be our guide and translator; and Myriam, who accompanies her.

Mother has three words of French. She has managed to say, 'Bonjour.' I didn't even know how to do that. Chékéba explains to us that for security reasons there are no cameras or photographers at the airport. All three of us shall have to go everywhere under borrowed names. From now on, I'm to be Latifa. That will be the name under which I'll sign my testimony.

Our first image of Paris, as we leave the airport, is of high rises, higher than any I've seen except in the movies. After that, it's the Eiffel Tower. I had imagined Paris as magnificent and it is just that.

We're launched into a whirlwind of activity: first there's the hotel, then a television programme. I'm reassured that my face will be blurred on the screen and unidentifiable. I'm shy to begin with, as Chékéba translates my responses to questions.

The next day, we take the train to go to the European Parliament in Brussels. Mother, Diba and I have become ambassadors for our poor country.

Chékéba tells me about the visit of Commander Massoud to Paris. She knows far more than I do on the subject. Apparently he asked for humanitarian assistance from the Ministry of Foreign Affairs and only managed to get symbolic support. There was no promise of direct aid. At Strasbourg, where he saw the President of the European Parliament, Nicole Fontaine, he asked for neither arms nor foreign military help in Afghanistan, but for France's support for the Resistance against the Taliban's power so as to prevent them from negotiating a peace deal and arriving at a political settlement. Nicole Fontaine, on her side, considered Commander Massoud a privileged negotiator on the road to a peace process.

After that Massoud went to Brussels to meet the most important representative of Europe in matters of foreign affairs, Javier Solana.

Chékéba tells me that the support Massoud managed to get was pretty thin, but that a newspaper, the *Courrier International*, published an appeal he signed, in which he spelled out the problem of the slippery frontier between Pakistan and Afghanistan, talked of the escalation of Pakistan's power in the region and its designs on Afghanistan, its wish to turn the country into a satellite state so that it can have a direct route to Central Asia.

Chékéba shows me a few extracts from this text of Massoud's:

> The Taliban massacred thousands of people because of their ethnic or religious affiliation. This is ethnic cleansing on a major scale . . . Afghanistan is facing a profound tragedy which could spark a regional conflagration, particularly since the Pakistanis and the Taliban maintain and form a whole terrorist underground which threatens neighbouring countries. I would have hoped that after our victory over the Communists, there would be some gratitude shown toward us and that aid would come to assuage our wounds. Unfortunately Pakistan stabbed us in the back, Washington put its trust in Islamabad, and Europe chose indifference. To put an end to this tragedy, the international community could, on the one hand, increase its humanitarian aid to the Afghan people, and on the other, apply pressure on Pakistan to stop its interference in Afghan affairs.

While the men talked politics, Mother, Diba and I could only speak of women, the oppressed who lived without voice or rights, designated victims of a systematic purification. Never again to work, to learn, to be seen. To be widows or beggars in our country where the men have been decimated by twenty years of war, are dead or handicapped or in exile, and have no more arms to oppose the Taliban.

One day, who knows, this purification will attain its height and we will all become women who have submitted to the ultimate decadence of a country so ancient and once so proud: we will become mothers forced to give birth to the sons of the Taliban. We must all three of us fight to say that we refuse to lose our dignity in this way, that we want to bring back from France a freedom that I have never known in twenty years of existence. We are a proud people. Our country is rich in history. I want to help to bring it the freedom it deserves.

Chékéba and our little group in burqas visit important people: Nicole Fontaine, Raymond Forni at the National Assembly, Christian Poncelet at the Senate, and Mr Josselin, the Minister for Cooperation.

My parents, Diba and I arrived in Paris on 2 May 2001. We were meant to leave ten days later, but our 'ambassadorial' visits lasted longer than we had expected, and we had to ask for our visas to be extended.

But by the end of May, I am distraught. If I hadn't met the journalists on *Elle* magazine, if I hadn't seen them cry, protest along the streets, support us, love us, I would almost regret this ambassadorial mission we've undertaken. I have the feeling nothing will ever change. My father, always optimistic, never stops repeating what good fortune we've had, being able to visit France, to meet all these people. On top of it, he says, words are never lost in the desert. One day they'll take root and flower.

'You haven't done this in vain,' he says to me. 'Trust me. Women listen to other women. Your testimony will make people here understand what the Taliban have imposed on us. Women aren't nothing. If a Talib says to a woman that she's nothing and he's everything, it's because he's ignorant. Men are born of women. The holiest man has a mother; the whole world was born from woman. You would do well to remember the Afghan proverb: "If the pearl can say to the oyster that she's nothing and that it's the one who does everything, then the fish can tell the sky to stop raining."'

On the last day of May, there's a fax for us from Daoud at the Embassy. He went to Pakistan to send it. He forewarns us that the Taliban have issued a fatwa against all women who denounce the regime. When he returned to Kabul, he learned that the Taliban had laid waste to our apartment. He didn't go to check it out. In fact, the neighbours alerted him that the Taliban had moved into it.

We've now lost everything. All our memories, our family photos, my uncle's paintings that my mother had hidden away so carefully. Nothing is left of our family in the borough of Mikrorayan.

My parents' eyes, fixed on the emptiness which is now our past, pierce my heart. I feel guilty. We can no longer go back to Kabul.

An Embassy employee confirms the disaster.

'They launched a fatwa against you without even knowing who you were. They say that these women who are in France talk only lies and that if they come back, they'll be killed. The text has made the rounds on the internet.'

When I think of all the risks that we took in order to get here! This time even my father is demoralized.

'Of course you were well received in France,' he now admits, 'but what good has it led to?'

I'm beside myself. From now on, life is a wandering in search of renewed visas, of lodging with other refugees. The questions go round and round in our heads with no answers. Am I here, alive? But what will become of me? I'm in a country where I don't speak the language. Mother is lost, mute in her world of suffering and misfortune. My father has lost everything. Two of his children are in Pakistan; another is in Russia; another in the United States. The family has broken apart, grown dispersed. I am the only one with them, the last of their daughters. How will I ever be able to take up my studies again? Where will we live? How to begin again? And begin what?

But the future will prove that we're not alone. We are the beneficiaries of the support of the Afghan community, of our Embassy, and of course, of our journalist friends who help us solve the problems of papers and lodgings.

I am given the opportunity to write a book – the hope of being able to explain how and why I reached the place where I find myself today.

Me. A young girl from Kabul, educated under the Soviet occupation, then during the time of the Communist governments that succeeded each other through four years of civil war, before finding herself imprisoned by a monstrous power and seeing her life confiscated at the age of sixteen.

Other Afghanis are still at war in my country. The refugees on the frontiers of the countries neighbouring Afghanistan suffer far more than I do. I'm well aware of that. What else is there for me to do but to tell the story of my life as a woman citizen of Kabul of which there is nothing left but ruins?

10 September 2001. Commander Massoud in his refuge at Panshir is the victim of suicide assassins, dressed as journalists. No one knows if he is dead or alive.

11 September. The very heart of America is attacked.

13 September. Ahmed Shah Massoud's death is announced.

7 October. American and Allied forces go to war against the Taliban.

I finish my modest tale at the hour when guns begin to speak in my place. They always have.

Azadi means freedom in our language. But who speaks Afghani?

I no longer know.

Glossary

Chador/Chadri Generally, a cloak or long scarf with which some Muslim women cover their head and shoulders. The heavier version is a garment of a sombre colour and composed of an opaque material sewn into a bonnet and a veil. Embroidered grillwork covers the eye area. Of various lengths, the garment can cover the arms or go all the way down to the feet. In Afghanistan the longer version is also called a **burqa**. (Until the 1980s this was used only by women in outlying provinces.)

Fatwa The response given to a legal question by a recognized authority in the Muslim community. This ruling, having the status of a decree, can rise to the issuing of a death sentence.

Jihad A sacred war to defend Islam or Muslims. In a prior meaning, jihad is the 'effort' that Muslims make to perfect themselves on an individual moral and religious plane.

Mahram A woman's male guardian, who can be her father, brother, husband, or in extreme cases, her cousin.

Mullah A religious authority.

176

Glossary

Mujahidin (singular Mujahid) Fighters for the faith; members of the Afghani Islamic Resistance during the Soviet Occupation (1979–89).

Pakol The traditional Afghani beret.

Pashtuns The largest ethnic group in Afghanistan, a country torn apart by the rivalry between its various ethnic groupings which also include the Hazars, Uzbeks, Tajiks and Turkimans.

Sharia The body of legal commandments drawn from the sacred texts of Islam, which rule the religious, political, social and personal life of Muslims.

Taliban (singular **Talib**) Religious students. In the case of Afghanistan in the 1990s, militants trained in Pakistani Koranic schools. These schools or **madrases** are part of the **Deobandi** school of thought. This orthodox strain of Islam, which preaches purification from all foreign influence, is an extremely narrow reading of the Koranic message. It was founded at the end of the nineteenth century in Deoband in the north of India and upheld by the British who wanted a religious power that could provide a counter-force to Hinduism.

Afterword

A Dream of Peace and Democracy

The black turbans of the Taliban are slowly disappearing from our nightmares: now it's important that we talk about hope and about freedom – finally found again. I'm doing just that.

From the moment I heard the laughter in Kabul, watched the face of a woman on television, saw that the barbers' razors were at work once more, I've known that I must go back and hug my country to myself. I'm only waiting for the kites to replace the bombers in the sky above Kandahar.

There is much to be happy about at the Bonn Conference: the promises of the representatives of each ethnic group – the Tajiks, Uzbeks, Pashtuns, Hazari – to dutifully rally behind a provisional government and to accept UN aid in the reconstruction of our country, a country devastated to an extent rarely seen in history. I do rejoice.

Wahid now longs to leave Moscow and go home. Daoud and his wife, and Soraya are all somewhere on the road between Pakistan and Afghanistan: we haven't heard from them for a long time and I worry.

As for me, I am for the moment a privileged exile who eats her fill, has no fears about the winter cold, and can hold her own with Westerners. So I can now express, without fear, my instinctive anxieties for the future – and that too is a privilege.

For centuries the men of my country have been given knives, guns, rifles, kalachnikovs to be played with like children's rattles. For centuries the rhythm of the generations has been played out like a chess game, grand masters succeeding each other, one after another, as if tribal wars were a national sport. For centuries, too, women were born to wear the burqa. And the ambitions of international powers supported these traditions.

I want to say – along with all my hopes for the dream of peace and democracy, to which my generation is ardently committed – that I pray that women will be more substantially represented in future debates. Out of the thirty people in Bonn, three women is not enough. I also pray that the man who leads our country will be, in his heart, as Pashtun as he is Tajik, Uzbek or Hazari; that his wife will advise him and assist him; that he will understand that he must surround himself with our best and wisest. I pray that books will replace arms; that education will lead us to respect one another; that hospitals will fulfill their mission; and that our culture will rise again from the ashes of our pillaged and burnt-out museums. I pray, too, that the camps full of starving refugees will disappear from our frontiers, and that soon the bread they eat will be baked by their own hands, in their own homes.

Praying won't be enough. As soon as the last Taliban has hung up his black turban and I can be a free woman in a free country, I'll return to my life in Afghanistan and take up my duties as a citizen, a woman – and I hope, one day, as a mother.

One day a European woman quoted from a song for me: 'Woman is the future of man.' In Afghanistan, more than anywhere else, I pray that soon men, too, will sing these words.

December 2001